THE
RIDING
HANDBOOK

A FIREFLY BOOK

Published by Firefly Books Ltd. 2007

Copyright © 2007 Marshall Editions

First printing

Publisher Cataloging-in-Publication Data (U.S.)

St. Aubyn, Zoe.
  The riding handbook : the complete guide to safe and exciting riding / Zoe St. Aubyn.
  [192] p. : col. ill., col. photos. ; cm.
  Includes index.
  Summary: The fundamentals of riding, including exercises and practice programs.
  ISBN-13: 978-1-55407-279-8 (pbk.)
  ISBN-10: 1-55407-279-4 (pbk.)
  1. Horsemanship. I. Title.
  798.23 dc22   SF309.S737 2007

Library and Archives Canada Cataloguing in Publication

St. Aubyn, Zoe
  The riding handbook : the complete guide to safe and exciting riding / Zoe St. Aubyn.
  Includes index.
  ISBN-13: 978-1-55407-279-8
  ISBN-10: 1-55407-279-4
  1. Horsemanship. I. Title.
  SF309.S73 2007   797.2'3
  C2007-900262-5

Published in the United States by
Firefly Books (U.S.) Inc.
P.O. Box 1338, Ellicott Station
Buffalo, New York 14205

Published in Canada by
Firefly Books Ltd.
66 Leek Crescent
Richmond Hill, Ontario L4B 1H1

Conceived, edited and designed in the
United Kingdom by:
Marshall Editions
The Old Brewery
6 Blundell Street
London N7 9BH
www.quarto.com

Publisher: Richard Green
Commissioning editor: Claudia Martin
Senior designer: Sarah Robson
Project editor: Johanna Geary
Editorial and design: Hart McLeod
Production: Nikki Ingram

Front cover photograph: Patrick Stubbs
www.naturalexpressions.co.uk

Originated in Hong Kong by Modern Age
Printed in China by Midas Printing
  International Limited

THE
RIDING
HANDBOOK

The complete guide to riding horses and ponies

ZOE ST. AUBYN

FIREFLY BOOKS

CONTENTS

INTRODUCTION

Equestrianism is a sport on the increase. It is a great social sport and is one of the few where men and women can compete on equal terms. Riding can be started at any age and can very easily offer a lifetime of enjoyment for the whole family.

Many people spend years attending riding clubs for regular lessons, while there are those who buy a horse and learn the ropes together. Whatever level you are at, there is always room for improvement, new skills to learn and better methods of achieving your goal.

Horses are often portrayed as complex animals—but this is not really true. They are very intelligent and, with the right level of understanding and training, they are totally co-operative. Their size makes them potentially dangerous so we, as humans, try to control and direct them in order to keep the upper hand.

Horses like routine and continuity—and these are good discipline for us as well. Having a horse or pony is not all about the riding: the stable management and what we do on the ground will set the standard for much of the ridden work.

From a very young age I was enrolled in the Pony Club and our local riding club. Through both, I learned valuable lessons in horse and pony care and riding skills. Over the years I was able to take part in every discipline with a variety of ponies. I never had any fear but I did have huge respect for my animals and took the time to bond with them. It is fair to say that there are a lot more "gadgets" around today to assist the rider. In reality, though, there is no substitute for a good basis of knowledge both on and off the horse.

I hope that this book will enable you to enjoy the sport of riding and owning your own horse to the utmost. It offers key advice on all of the important areas that you need to know about and aims to give you a desire to take your riding to the next level.

Zoe St. Aubyn

KNOWING YOUR HORSE

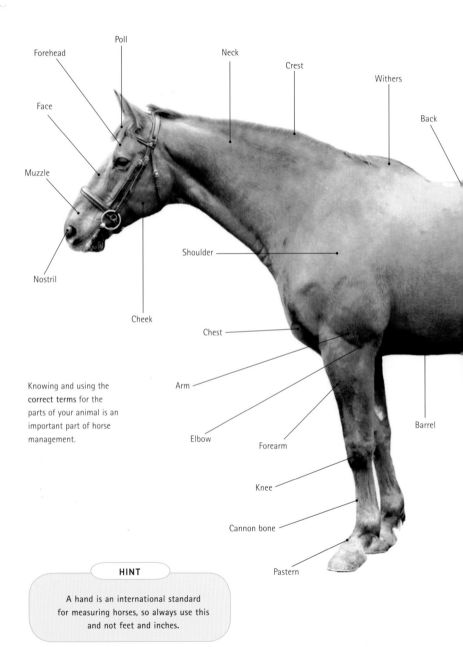

Poll

Forehead

Neck

Crest

Withers

Face

Back

Muzzle

Nostril

Shoulder

Cheek

Chest

Knowing and using the
correct terms for the
parts of your animal is an
important part of horse
management.

Arm

Barrel

Elbow

Forearm

Knee

Cannon bone

Pastern

HINT

A hand is an international standard
for measuring horses, so always use this
and not feet and inches.

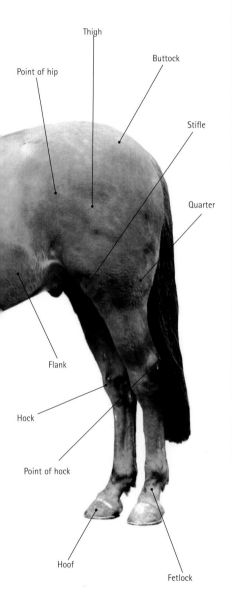

Thigh

Buttock

Point of hip

Stifle

Quarter

Flank

Hock

Point of hock

Hoof

Fetlock

HORSE AND PONY MEASUREMENTS

Horses and ponies are measured from the ground to the highest point of their withers. The traditional unit of measurement is the "hand"—this comes from the practice of measuring horses using the width of a man's hand, which averaged 4 in (10 cm).

A horse's height is described as being x hands high, such as 16 hands high, but it is typical to shorten this to 16hh. When the height is over a number of hands, such as 16 hands and 2 in, it is referred to as 16.2hh.

Horses measure over 14.2hh, while ponies measure 14.2hh and under. When measuring them, make sure the animal can stand squarely on solid, level ground as this will give the most accurate measurement. A special measuring stick should be used for this purpose.

Standing next to the shoulder and facing away from the horse's head, hold the measuring stick a short distance from the horse and lower the crossbar onto the withers. Ensure that the crossbar is level in order to achieve an **accurate height measurement**.

ASSESSING CONFORMATION

Conformation can be described as the shape or body structure of a horse, with particular attention paid to proportion and skeletal structure.

A horse with good conformation should have an overall balance of features, with each part being in proportion to the others. This not only results in a horse that is pleasing to the eye, but also has an important impact on its overall health and well-being. Good conformation enables a horse to be balanced and less prone to strain or injury.

Head
The head must be in proportion with the body. A large head will affect the horse's balance, making it carry more weight on its front, that is, be on its forehand.

Head sizes will vary depending on the breed, but good bone structure and a kind eye are important starting points.

A slightly convex profile (Roman nose) may indicate some common breeding, such as in a cob, whereas a concave, "dished" face will indicate Arab or Welsh breeding.

It is important that the head is set on the neck at a good angle as this will affect breathing and the ability to flex in ridden work. A horse with a thick-set jowl or a large amount of flesh through the jowl area will find working correctly very difficult.

Eyes
The eyes should be large, clear, bright and well set on either side of the head. Although not scientifically proven, small eyes are thought to suggest a mean streak or stubbornness, while an excess of white around the color of the eye may suggest some wildness or bad temper.

Neck
The neck should be muscular and well set onto the shoulders. A short, thick neck indicates a lot of power and is seen in heavier horses, such as cobs. A long, arched neck indicates elegance and can be seen in breeds such as the thoroughbred.

Shoulders
The shoulders should be well muscled with a good slope. A straight shoulder often produces a short stride and a choppy "up and down" movement, which can give a jarring, uncomfortable ride. However, it is quite desirable in a number of driving breeds.

Forelegs
The forelegs should be well muscled through the forearm, and good length in this upper leg is essential for speed. Knees should be broad and flat with no puffiness or lumps. The cannon bones should be flat at the front and preferably short rather than long. This ensures that the tendons at the back of the bone are short and less likely to damage. The pastern should be of medium length and good slope. Too much slope puts strain on the tendon and too straight absorbs less concussion, which gives a less comfortable ride.

A horse that has all, or most, of the **key conformation points** will almost certainly ride well too.

Feet

The feet must be of good quality. The two front feet and the two hind feet should each look like a matching pair and point forward. The angle of the hoof wall should continue the line from the slope of the pastern. On the underside of the foot there should be a good-quality, clean frog, and the bars of the foot should be wide and deep.

Chest and barrel

The chest should be deep and have enough room for a pair of clippers to pass between the front legs. If too wide, it may produce a rolling action when ridden. The ribs should be well sprung and give a rounded appearance. This is important in order to provide adequate space for heart and lungs and for lung expansion during hard exercise. For this reason, there should also be plenty of depth in the girth, that is, from the withers to behind the elbow. The back should be level, short, strong and muscular.

Hindquarters

The hindquarters should be well muscled and the tail set on fairly high. The thigh muscles on the inside of the hind legs should be well developed so that the horse does not appear to split up the middle. There should be a reasonable amount of length from the point of hip to the point of hock. The hock joint should be large but not fleshy and not show any signs of swelling. The line from the point of the hock down the back of the leg should be straight and not bulge over the joint.

> **HINT**
>
> In addition to satisfying technical points, any horse you buy or ride should give you a good gut feeling. An expert's opinion will help.

POOR CONFORMATION

Ewe neck

Neck

A neck that is upside-down with no crest and a bulky lower line is known as a "ewe" neck. In ridden work, a ewe neck makes it difficult for the rider to achieve the correct head carriage and also gives the horse a more hollow back, especially when jumping, thus hindering good forward movement. A ewe neck can sometimes be the fault of bad schooling and can be altered with correct training.

Forelegs

* *Back at the knee.* Viewed from the side, the whole foreleg appears concave, slightly bending toward the hind legs. This is a bad conformation as it puts a great deal of strain on the back tendons.

* *Over at the knee.* This is the reverse of "back at the knee"—it is a preferable condition as there is less strain on the tendons. However, too much forward bend will make the horse prone to tripping or stumbling.

* *Knock-kneed or bow-legged.* From the front, the knees turn inward or outward respectively. A horse with this problem will not move straight.

* *Pigeon-toed.* The toes turn inward.

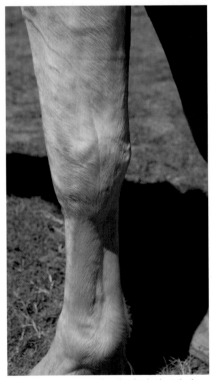

Leg showing **back at the knee**

Cow hocks

Back
- *Dip or sway back.* Although horses with this conformation are often comfortable to ride, an unduly dipped back is weak and can be prone to muscle problems and potential ligament strains.

- *Roach back.* This is an upward curve in the back. It can make saddle-fitting difficult.

Hocks
- *Sickle hocks.* Overbent hocks that cause the cannon bone to slant.

- *Cow hocks.* Hocks that point toward each other cause the legs to move outward instead of forward.

- *Bowed hocks.* Hocks that turn outward.

Feet
- *"Boxy" feet.* Upright feet that are best avoided.

- *Flat feet.* Feet that have a flat sole are always weak. They bruise easily and are prone to corns.

Dipped back

CHOOSING THE RIGHT HORSE

Straightness and soundness are important factors to look for when buying a horse.

The first steps

When buying a horse or pony, it is important to take into account the following factors:

- Your ability—are you a novice rider looking for a safe horse to gain experience or a more competent rider looking to take part in competitions?
- Your circumstances—do you have your own land or will you need to keep your horse at a boarding facility? Will you ride every day or just on weekends?
- The extent of your knowledge—if you are keen to own a horse but have limited knowledge, take an experienced rider or instructor with you to assess an animal.

It is useful to take some time to decide on a profile of a suitable horse.

Points for you to consider when choosing include:

- What breed or type of horse or pony do you want?
- What age range?
- What price are you expecting to pay?
- What experience should the horse have had?
- What type of riding are you intending to do?
- Would you prefer owning a mare or gelding?

Watching a horse being ridden by another rider can help you to assess whether it will be a suitable ride for you.

Viewing a prospective purchase

When assessing a horse or pony for purchase, ask the owners to trot them in a straight line away from, and back toward you. By observing whether the horse moves evenly and straight, you can assess its soundness and ability to move correctly. Look out for signs of dishing (front legs swinging outward), plaiting (legs crossing in front of each other) and brushing (legs moving too close together).

Stand back from the horse and look it over from head to tail. Next, run your hand down the neck, over the withers and check for any signs of pain or discomfort. Continue down the legs, checking for heat, hard lumps or soft swellings that could indicate signs of injury.

An inspection by a qualified veterinarian.

Next, watch the horse being tacked up and note how it behaves. Does it stand still and accept this willingly or are there signs of tension, biting or kicking?

It is preferable to see the horse being ridden by the owner before riding it yourself. This gives you the chance to assess its attitude to work, its level of training and obedience to its rider. Ask to see walk, trot and canter on both the left and the right reins. If you intend to do some jumping, watch the horse go over a few jumps first. If you feel that you would now like to ride the horse, remember that the owner will be very used to the animal and you should take some time in walk to get a feel for it and check that you are able to start, stop and steer before moving on to faster paces.

Buying the horse

If you think you have found the right animal and wish to buy it, it is advisable to have the horse checked ("vetted") by a qualified veterinarian, preferably one specializing in horses, before closing the deal. A veterinarian will provide a thorough inspection of the horse and advise you on its suitability for the type of riding you wish to do.

HINT

Buying a horse can be a lengthy process, but if you are going to find the right one, be prepared to take your time.

THE HORSE'S LANGUAGE

Horses use body language as their main form of communication. They use a wide range of signals that they clearly understand among themselves. Their ability to read body movements is highly developed and much better than that of a human. This allows them to work together as a herd to avoid predators as well as to detect small changes in a rider's body that are given as instructions.

As riders and handlers, we need to understand what the horse is trying to tell us in order to help it and to prevent any potential harm or injury to ourselves.

Kicking is a natural defense mechanism used to warn others.

Kicking

A horse that kicks is rarely welcome but horses use kicking as one of their main defense mechanisms. The signs that a horse may be about to kick are the ears being laid back and the horse swinging its hindquarters toward you. Horses have a very good reach with the back legs and a lot of power—a kick using both hind legs can cause a lot of damage. Horses also have the ability to kick out sideways (cow kick) with one leg. It is important to avoid situations that could make a horse feel obliged to defend itself. Never put yourself in danger—always ensure that you read the horse's body language and stand out of range.

A **swishing tail** may come before a kick or buck—rider beware!

Biting

Some horses may just nip, but if they are inclined to bite, this could be because such habits were not checked as a foal, or they are frightened or defending themselves. A biting horse is never popular and steps need to be taken to stop or avoid this.

A horse may also bite in response to pain. If a horse threatens to bite as you place the saddle, it may be trying to tell you that it has pain or discomfort in its back. Problems with the fit of the saddle may be causing soreness in the muscles, or the girth may pinch when it is done up, causing discomfort.

Tail swishing

Swishing the tail is another sign that a horse is angry or annoyed and can be a precursor to kicking out or bucking.

Ears

A horse's ears have a wide range of movement and are used constantly to monitor what is going on around them. They are a good indicator for riders and handlers of where the horse's attention is focused and also of mood. Forward or pricked ears may signify that a horse is concentrating on something, being inquisitive, alert or startled. Ears laid flat back can mean the horse is frightened, angry or being aggressive.

Alert ears and eyes are a good sign of a keen horse.

17

GENERAL HANDLING

Safety is the first and most important consideration when handling your horse—safety for yourself, your horse and anyone around you. Horses are much stronger than humans and boundaries need to be set so that they know their limits.

In the stable
Always let the horse know that you are approaching the stable. If surprised or alarmed, even a good-tempered horse may react violently—kicking out for example. If it is standing near the stable door when you wish to enter, insist that the horse moves back when asked. When in the stable, it should be taught to move its quarters over when requested, in order to give you room to move around. If it turns its back to you, do not chase it around the stable. Instead, turn your own back to the horse and it will soon become inquisitive and turn around. When leading it out of the stable, insist that it waits until the door is opened wide enough to exit and then ask it to walk out calmly. A horse that barges from its stable may injure itself or you.

A horse being led correctly.

Leading safely
Most horses are safe enough to lead in a halter, especially when in their home surroundings. In some circumstances, such as when a horse is fresh, unknown to you, or you are in a public place, it is advisable to use a bridle. A bridle gives you more control over the horse as it tends to respect the bit in its mouth.

Generally, a horse is led from its left side, although it is always sensible to ensure that the horse leads from either side. Your right hand should hold the lead rope near to the halter and your left hand takes up the rest of the rope. When leading in a bridle, take the reins over the neck and hold them firmly in both hands, about 10–12 in (25–30 cm) from the bit.

Catching and turning out
When catching a horse, walk into the field and approach the horse quietly and calmly. Some horses will walk toward you to be caught, while others remain eating and wait for you to walk to them. If you have to approach, make sure that the horse has seen you and knows you are coming. Remain calm, placing the lead rope around its neck and then putting on the halter. Lead the horse quietly and steadily to the gate.

When turning out a horse, lead it into the field, walking on its left. Make sure it stands while you either unclip the lead rope—if leaving the halter on—or gently and quietly remove the halter. When the horse is loose,

A horse tied up properly in a stable.

do not flap your arms or smack it with the halter to send it on into the field, as this will teach the horse to bolt or possibly kick out.

Tying up

A horse must *always* be tied up using a quick-release knot. Never tie up a horse in a way that cannot be undone speedily if the circumstances dictate. A horse that is startled or frightened while tied up may panic and pull back, which could result in damage to itself, people or property.

Always release the halter slowly to avoid any erratic behavior.

THE QUICK RELEASE KNOT

1
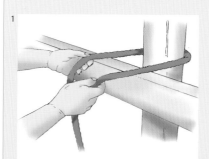

Pass the rope around the post or ring. Hold the two parts loosely. The loose end should be in your right hand and the snap in your left.

2
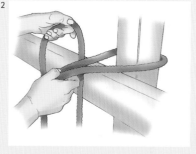

Then take both parts in your right hand and pass the long end, looped, under the snap end.

3

Make a loop with the long end and take the rope back over the snap and pull through the circle.

4

Pull tight against the post or ring. A pull on the snap end ensures quick release.

RELATIONSHIP BUILDING

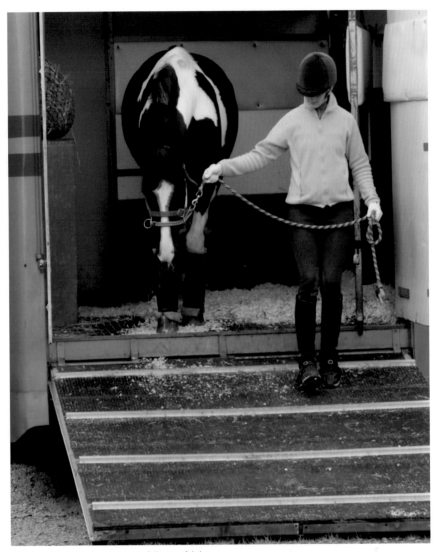

Arriving at their new home—a potentially stressful time.

Relationship building is an area that should not be overlooked when acquiring a new horse or pony. In our haste to get started with our new animal, we often forget the stress it is under in its new situation. Imagine yourself moving to a new house: it can take a while to familiarize yourself with your new surroundings and neighbors. It is the same for a horse moving to a new home. It has to learn about this new environment, find its place in the hierarchy of a new herd, establish new friendship bonds, adapt to a new daily routine and, most importantly, learn to communicate with and trust a new owner.

Riding
In addition, you will probably be keen to tack up and go riding right away. If the horse is used to being ridden on a daily basis, then starting ridden work immediately can help give continuity to its routine. If this is not the case, then give the horse some time to settle into its new environment.

In the stable
Spend as much time as possible with the horse in any activity that involves contact and conversation:

- Be with the horse in the stable—this can be just talking to it or mucking out.
- Tie up the horse outside its stable and let it enjoy being groomed; pull or plait its mane and tail.

Your objective is to understand and know your horse better, and its objective is to trust you and relax into its new home.

Outside the stable
Try taking the horse for a walk, but for safety reasons make sure to do this in a bridle, possibly attaching a lead rope to the bridle as an additional precaution. When walking,

Riding is important but **don't be in too much of a hurry.**

talk to the horse and occasionally stroke it. Be calm and positive in your approach to give it as much confidence and reassurance as possible. If you have any safe areas, let it graze for a while.

In the field
If your new horse is to be turned out, make sure that you have checked the field beforehand. Repair any loose or unsafe fencing, remove any unwanted plants, such as ragwort, and walk around the field looking for any objects that could cause damage. Try to check on your new horse regularly, especially if turned out with other horses.

Try to spend some time watching it in the field—you can learn many things about your horse's nature in this way. You could maximize the use of your time by also doing some mucking.

Feeling at home
These simple ideas can help a horse to settle into its new home, so when tacking up and going for a ride, it will feel at home and familiar with its new environment.

Spend as much time with your new horse as possible.

BONDING EXERCISES

Take the time to **trace your hand over your horse's body** to relax you both and gain a better understanding.

Bonding with your horse should start on your first day and continue throughout your life together. The more the two of you bond, the better you get to know, understand and trust each other.

Bonding in the stable

A good early bonding exercise is to run your hand over all of your horse's body. Using the palm of your hand, start at the ears and trace your hand over the whole face, stroking over the eyes, down the nose to the nostrils, and then back up under its chin before going down the neck.

While slowly moving your hand over your horse, you may discover some areas of sensitivity or some where it particularly enjoys being touched—you can focus on these each day. Some horses are sensitive on the girth area behind the elbow or under the belly and may try to bite or kick to avoid

these areas being touched; others enjoy being scratched around the withers or near the base of the tail.

Work your hand over the shoulders, going across the girth area and down the front legs. Move to the underbelly and continue toward the hindquarters. When handling the hindquarters and legs, stand to the side and not directly behind the horse. If you accidentally alarm it or the horse reacts adversely to you touching a particular place, you need to be in the safest position possible to avoid injury to either yourself or the horse.

Bonding in hand

Another excellent bonding exercise can be done in hand. With the horse in a halter, hold the lead rope at least 20 in (50 cm) from the clip and ask him to walk alongside you. After several steps, stop and stand still. Do not give him any voice commands but watch him to check if he also stops. Ideally, he should follow your lead and stop when you do. If he does not stop, take a couple more steps and stop again. If he still fails to stop, a couple of light tugs on the lead rope may be needed to get your message across. If he turns in to face you when you stop, correct this immediately by turning him back into the direction you were going.

When you have established the halt, turn around so that you are facing the horse. Put the lead rope in your left hand and with your right hand press your fingers on the front of his chest. He should walk backward from the pressure of your hand, just a couple of steps. Ideally, he should move

from the lightest touch from you, although such lightness may take a little time to establish. Turn yourself around, take up the lead rope again, and walk on, stopping again in a few strides. Repeat the correctional aid if he continues to walk on when you have stopped. Once he has understood your needs, try this in trot. Ideally, there should be no need to use the voice as your actions should be all he needs, but you may need to use some vocal commands to support your actions initially if he does not understand what you require of him.

This exercise can be particularly useful in the early days and really helps you both to start working in harmony together.

A bonding exercise involves the handler **touching the horse's chest** to move him backward.

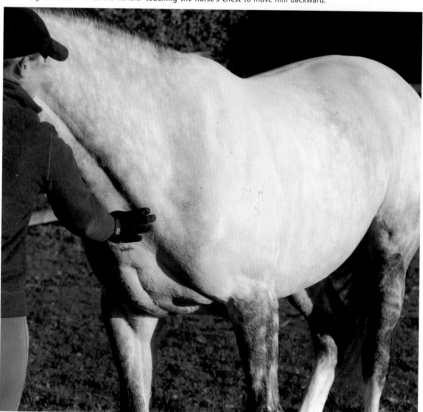

■ ENGLISH TACK

To ride safely and securely, two items of tack are essential for the full enjoyment of riding—a saddle and a bridle. After the purchase of your horse, these are probably the next expensive items you have to buy.

Saddles and bridles can be bought ready made, but it is also possible to have a saddle-maker make a saddle especially for your horse. While this can be a more expensive option, the saddle will be made to the exact measurements of your horse, giving it maximum comfort and you maximum control.

Saddles

There are many different types of saddles available to suit the wide variety of today's equestrian activities. For everyday riding, the most commonly used saddle is the general purpose. As its name suggests, it is designed to be used for jumping, hacking and schooling. For riders specializing in dressage, the dressage saddle has a deeper seat and straighter flaps than the general purpose to give the rider optimum balance in the saddle and enable them to sit in the most central position to perform dressage movements. For show-jumping, the jumping saddle has forward-cut flaps to accommodate the rider's leg at the shorter stirrup length needed for jumping position.

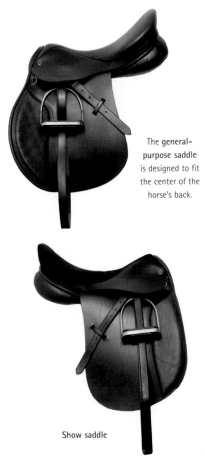

The **general-purpose saddle** is designed to fit the center of the horse's back.

Jumping saddle

Dressage saddle

Show saddle

GIRTHS

These girths are all shaped to help prevent **girth galls**.

The function of the girth is to hold the saddle in place. Its design will depend on the horse's conformation and the type of work being done. The best and most durable are the leather girths—the Balding, Atherstone and Threefold. They will last a long time if well looked after and look very sharp for competitions. Today, girths are also available in synthetic materials. Girths should be cleaned and checked for wear regularly to avoid any potential rubbing or sores.

Bridles

As for saddles, there are a variety of bridles available. They come in three standard sizes—pony, cob, or full. Ideally they should be of good-quality leather but are also available in synthetic materials. Ideally, the bridle should match the color of the saddle. The standard colors are light brown, dark brown or black. Try to select a bridle where the color and width of the leather complements your horse or pony. Horses, particularly hunter types, look better with wider leather, whereas the smaller head of a show pony or Arab suits a much finer, lighter leather.

Nosebands

Nosebands are also available in various designs. The cavesson is the most common and is largely used for appearance only—many people feel it "finishes off" the look of the horse's head. Other nosebands, such as the drop, flash and grackle, are designed to give the rider more control. They do this by preventing the horse from evading the bit, which it might try to do by opening its mouth or crossing its jaw.

The basic noseband should sit just below the cheek bones and be fastened without any slack at the back of the jaw.

Double bridle

Cavesson noseband

Grackle noseband

Flash noseband

HINT

Try to combine look, quality, and comfort when buying tack.
Recycled or secondhand tack can be a good starting point.

FITTING AN ENGLISH SADDLE

A good fit

The importance of selecting an English saddle that is properly fitted to you and your horse cannot be underestimated. A poor-fitting saddle will cause discomfort and possible injury to the horse's back. It will restrict the horse's movement and can lead to it bucking or resisting your aids in order to avoid pain caused by pressure from the saddle. The main points for checking the fit of a saddle are:

- It must be the right size for horse and rider.
- There must be no pressure on the horse's spine. There must be a clear channel through the gullet (the central groove on the saddle's underside).
- It must not press down on the withers. You should be able to fit at least two fingers between the withers and the arch below the pommel; nor should it pinch them—if the fit is too tight, a wider tree is needed.
- It must sit level and distribute the rider's weight evenly. It should not hamper the movement of the shoulders nor rest too far back on the loins.

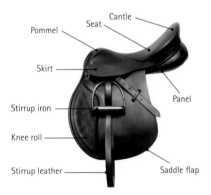

General-purpose English saddle

Pommel · Seat · Cantle · Skirt · Stirrup iron · Knee roll · Stirrup leather · Saddle flap · Panel

Placing a saddle

- Smooth down the hair where the saddle and girth will lie and check there is no mud or old sweat in the coat to cause sores.
- If you are using an unattached saddlecloth or numnah under the saddle, gently place it well forward on the horse's back and then slide it back into position.

- Pick up the saddle with your left hand holding the front arch and your right hand holding the cantle (back of the saddle).
- Stand at the horse's nearside (left side) shoulder; without too much of a swing that might scare the horse, lift the saddle over the horse's back and gently place it down.
- If you have a numnah attached to the saddle, place the saddle well forward near the withers and then slide it back into the correct position. Never slide a saddle forward as it will reverse the direction of the hair and cause the horse discomfort.
- Check to see that the saddle is neither too far forward on the shoulder nor too far back on the loins. It should rest flat on the horse's back and the seat should be level with the ground. The pommel (front arch of the saddle) should never be higher than the cantle, whereas the cantle will usually be noticeably higher than the pommel.
- Ensure any numnah is lying flat and is well pulled up into the front arch of the saddle. It should be covering all areas of the saddle in direct contact with the horse's back.

Doing up a girth

- Once the saddle is in place, go quickly but quietly to the offside (right side) and attach the girth (unless it is already fitted to the saddle), then gently lower it. Check that all is flat and smooth under the flap.
- Return to the nearside and reach under the stomach for the girth.
- Gently pull up toward the girth straps.
- Lift the saddle flap with your right arm so you can clearly see and do the girth up sufficiently but not too tight—remember that many horses can "blow out" when having their girths done up.
- The girth should be done up tight enough so that the saddle does not slip but not so tight as to cause the horse discomfort.

> **HINT**
>
> Keep all your tack clean and oiled. Supple saddles, bridles, reins, etc., are good for you and your horse.

Place the saddlecloth or numnah.

Check the saddle is in the correct place.

Reach for the girth.

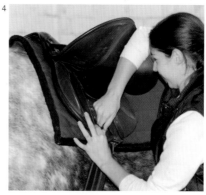

Lift the saddle flap with your right arm.

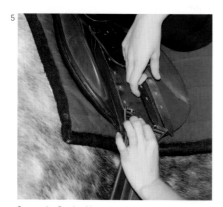

Secure the first buckle.

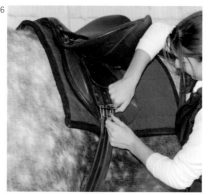

Secure the second buckle.

FITTING A BRIDLE

To use an English bridle effectively and safely, it must be correctly fitted to the horse's head by adjusting the length of each piece of the bridle.

- The browband should not be set so high that it rubs the front of the horse's ears nor be so tight that it rubs the back of the ears.
- The throatlash must not restrict breathing, so the width of four fingers should fit between the throatlash and the horse's cheek when at the correct length.
- The noseband should sit about two fingers' width below the cheek bones.
- For the bridle to be the correct length, the cheekpieces should be adjusted so that the bit is in contact with the corner of the mouth, causing it to form one wrinkle.
- The bit size must be correct for the width of the horse's mouth and should protrude ¼ inch (0.5 cm) on each side. If too narrow, it will pinch; if too wide, it may "saw" and cause soreness.

Without properly fitting the bridle to the horse's head, the horse will be very uncomfortable and riding will be unsafe.

Putting on a bridle
- Stand on the nearside of the horse's head.
- Place the reins over the head. If the horse is wearing a halter, undo it, remove from the head, and re-tie around the neck.
- Hold the top of the bridle in your right hand and slide the bridle up the horse's head.
- Use your left hand to guide the bit to the horse's mouth.
- Encourage the horse to open its mouth by gently squeezing with your thumb and fourth finger on the corners of the mouth.
- Gently slide the bit in its mouth while placing the headpiece over the ears.
- Ensure the bridle is siting comfortably by pulling the forelock through the browband, sitting the browband below the ears and adjusting the mane under the headpiece.
- Check that the bit is sitting correctly in the horse's mouth—the sides of the mouth should have one wrinkle.
- Do up the throatlash to the correct length.
- Fasten the noseband, allowing two fingers' width between it and the front of the face. This gives the horse the freedom to open its mouth slightly and to flex its jaw.
- If you are using a curbchain, this is the last piece you should do up. It should not hang loose but be done up so one finger can be placed between the chain and the horse's chin groove.
- Check the bridle is on straight, with the noseband and bits level.
- Undo the halter and slide away from the reins, making sure not to get anything caught up.

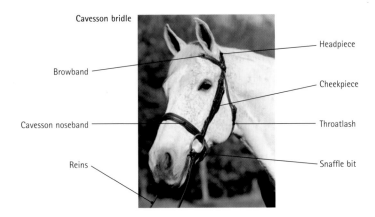

Cavesson bridle

Browband

Cavesson noseband

Reins

Headpiece

Cheekpiece

Throatlash

Snaffle bit

PUTTING ON A BRIDLE

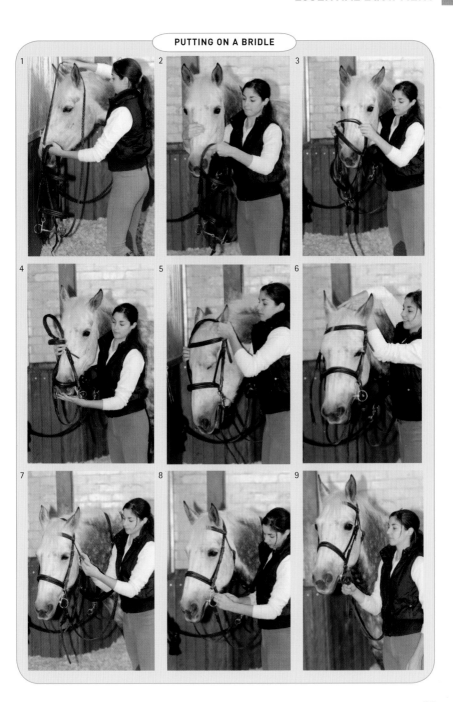

OTHER EQUIPMENT

In addition to the saddle and bridle, there is a range of other equipment available for the horse and rider, such as boots, spurs and breastplates. Always ask someone experienced for advice before purchasing equipment.

BOOTS

There are many different types of boots designed to prevent a horse injuring itself or being injured. A few are described below.

Brushing boots
Brushing boots, including fetlock boots and ring boots, can be fitted to both front and back legs. Their main purpose is to protect the inside of the leg from being struck by the opposite foot. Brushing boots are usually used for all-round protection against knocks and are generally fastened by Velcro straps.

Over-reach boots
Over-reach boots are bell-shaped and made of rubber. They fit around the lower part of the pastern and are used on the front feet to prevent the horse from over-reaching and injuring the front heel with the hind toe. These boots can be used for all sports and are commonly seen in jumping. Many horses are often turned out in over-reach boots since, as well as preventing injury, they also protect against shoes being pulled off.

Brushing exercise boot   Over-reach boot

Fetlock ring

Fetlock boot   Tendon boot

Tendon boots
These are designed give some support to the tendons and to provide protection against high over-reach.

Martingales

Martingales are designed to control head carriage. They are used in the jumping disciplines, such as show-jumping, eventing and hunting but are not allowed in dressage.

The two most common types of martingale, the standing and the running, are used to prevent the horse from raising its head too high and out of the angle of control. When the horse's head goes above the point of control, the martingale places pressure on the head so the horse cannot raise it higher. The martingale is also used to prevent a horse from rearing.

The standing martingale attaches to a cavesson noseband. A rubber stop at the neckstrap prevents the martingale from slipping forward.

Breastplates

Breastplates, breastcollars and breastgirths are used to prevent the saddle from sliding backward. They are usually seen in demanding, fast-paced sports such as eventing and show-jumping. They are also used in Western events, with a more decorative than utilitarian function.

Running martingale and breastplate: Rubber stops are placed on both reins between the bit and the rings of the running martingale to prevent the rings catching on the rein buckles.

Spurs

Spurs differ between Western and English-style riding. Western spurs usually have rowels and are designed to be used by running the rowel across the horse's side. The spurs are normally longer to accommodate the leg position of the Western rider, which is held off the side of the horse more than in English riding. English riders tend to use a spur that is shorter, as they merely turn their toe outward to activate the spur. The English spur should always be worn pointed downward, sitting on the boot's spur rest, with the buckle on the outside of the leg.

English spurs

Western spurs

WESTERN TACK

Tacked up and ready for Western riding.

The Western saddle is very different from the English saddle, being designed for the rider to spend hours in the saddle with minimum discomfort. The seat is very broad, and although the saddle is very heavy, the weight is spread over a large area. The stirrup leathers, known as "fenders," are long and broad, which makes long hours in the saddle more comfortable, and as they position the rider's leg off the horse, they also help to keep the horse's sweat away from the rider's legs.

Western saddles are secured by two girths called cinches. The front cinch lies behind the elbow, while the back cinch lies behind the rider's leg. The purpose of the back cinch is to keep the saddle in place, which is necessary for ranch work such as lassoing cattle. The front of the Western saddle has a horn that was developed for roping work. Once an animal is roped, the rope is fixed around the horn to prevent it from escaping; it is of ultimate importance that the saddle cannot move so that neither the horse nor the rider can be brought down.

Unlike an English saddle, most Western saddles fit most horses. This enabled ranch workers to use their saddle on any horse. One or two thick blankets are placed underneath the saddle to give added protection and comfort. Often, Western saddles are quite decorative and saddles used for competition can have a large quantity of silver ornamentation.

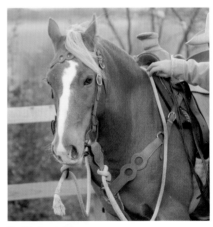

The Western bridle

FITTING A WESTERN SADDLE

1

Lay the blanket well forward on the horse's back, then slide it back into position.

2

Place the saddle on the back. Check that the blanket is lying evenly and lay the cinches and breastcollar over the seat. Hook the right stirrup over the saddle horn to prevent these from hitting the horse when the saddle is put in place.

3

Move around to the offside to gently let down the cinches and stirrup, then return to the nearside to secure the saddle. If you use a flank cinch, always tighten the front cinch first. Grasp the front cinch strap and put it through the cinch ring and saddle twice. Secure the buckle or tie a cinch knot.

4

Fasten the breastcollar—you may want to do this loosely now and tighten at the end.

5

Buckle the flank cinch just tight enough so that a hand can fit flat underneath it.

6

Once all the cinches are tightened, check the breastcollar and lower the stirrup.

THE A-Z OF BITS

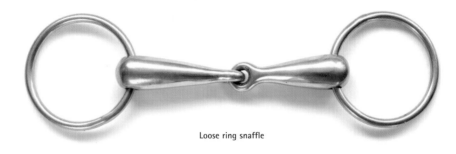

Loose ring snaffle

Selecting the right bit for your horse is possibly one of the most important elements for riding safely and ensuring control. Unsuitable bitting can ruin a horse's mouth permanently, but a rider with bad hands can do as much damage with the kindest bit as a harsh one.

A newly purchased horse may be sold with all their tack. If you find your new horse goes well with you in his old bit, then there is no need for change. If, however, you think you have a problem with control and/or direction, ask an expert to watch you ride and give advice. If possible, try borrowing some different bits to help you make a more informed choice.

How does a bit work?

Pressure from the hands via the reins puts pressure on the horse in a variety of ways, depending on the type of bit. The control points will either be the bars of the mouth, the tongue, the lips and corners of the mouth, the roof of the mouth, the curb groove, the poll or the nose.

Types of bits

Bits can be divided into four families—the snaffle, the double bridle, the pelham, and gadget-type bits. There are a large number of different bits within each bit family. Here are just a few examples:

- The **snaffle** is the most widely used family of bits as it contains bits that are the kindest to the horse and easiest to fit. A jointed snaffle gives a nutcracker effect and acts on the tongue, bars and corners of the mouth.
- The **double bridle** consists of a curb bit (Weymouth) and a bridoon (snaffle). It is used by more advanced riders and horses when more refined aids are needed. The bridoon raises the horse's head; engaging the curb bit puts pressure on the bars, tongue and poll and also the chin groove from the curbchain to create flexion at the poll.
- The **pelham** is a combination of a snaffle and curb in one mouthpiece. The upper ring takes the snaffle rein, allowing the bit to operate in the same way as a snaffle,

French link snaffle

Eggbutt snaffle

Weymouth with bridoon

Pelham

Weymouth double bridle

Kimblewick with curb

and the rein for the lower ring engages the curb.

- **Gadget-type** bits include the gag, the hackamore and the kimblewick with curb. The gag gives a rider more control over a strong horse. It is used with double reins— one rein goes direct to the bit ring, the other to the running cheeks. This allows it to be used either as a standard rein as a snaffle, or the second rein gives extra breaking power through the cheekpieces. The hackamore is a bitless bridle. The cheekpieces of the bit act as levers to put pressure on the nose, poll and chin groove.

Multi-ring/Dutch gag, hackamore

WORK CLOTHES

The versatility of equestrian clothing means that you can spend all day in the same clothes, whether working at the yard or riding.

The nature of working with horses dictates that the clothing you wear must be extremely practical at all times. The major considerations here are safety, practicality for cleaning and comfort. You will find that neat clothing that fits well but not too tightly is the easiest and most comfortable to move around in.

Legwear
Jodhpurs or jeans are the best options for working with horses, being both versatile and practical. Jodhpurs are available in a wide range of colors, but navy, brown or black are most practical for yard work. In warmer weather, shorts will help you keep cool if you are not planning to ride.

Neat, practical clothes enable you to carry out work in safety and comfort.

Tops

A large range of tops that are both fashionable and practical are available nowadays for any time of the year. In spring or autumn, the classic polo shirt or sweatshirt can be used under a lightweight jacket that comes complete with many pockets. In the winter months, choose from waterproof full-length riding coats to fully fitted, down-filled jackets for freezing, early-morning starts at the yard.

Footwear

It is very important that you wear suitable footwear at all times—a misplaced hoof can cause much damage to a handler's foot. Yard boots or leather jodhpur boots offer good protection. The soles usually have a good tread that gives secure footing when handling horses. Some boots are now available with protective toecaps. Do not wear open-toed shoes or sandals.

Cell phones

Cell phones are an almost essential item these days. Although they often reside inside pockets, there are now some cell phone holders available that are strong and waterproof and designed to be worn either on the arm or around the top of the calf to allow for easy access. If you need to be regularly available by phone, then another consideration is to use a hands-free set. It is difficult and not always safe to deal with a horse, either schooling or leading, if one hand is used for taking a call. With a hands-free phone everyone's safety is considered. Ensure you keep the ring volume down.

> **HINT**
>
> Horse work is dirty work.
> Don't wear your best clothes.

RIDING CLOTHES

Comfort and safety are major factors when riding your horse.

Hats
This is probably the most important piece of horsewear equipment that you will buy. Always buy a hat brand new—a used one could have unseen damage to the inner linings and will not provide the necessary protection. There are many different name brands of hats available in various styles and colors. Hats come in English and Western styles as well as sporty models for hacking and schooling (see also *Riding Hats*, pages 42–43).

Jodhpurs
Jodhpurs are always the best option for riding as they are designed to fit the body and there is no excess fabric that could cause rubbing or soreness. They are made from very durable material that will withstand many washes before needing to be repaired or replaced. They are also available with suede knee pads and/or seat that help to give extra grip when riding.

Chaps
Chaps are a good alternative to full-length boots. They come in full- and half-length and are usually made of leather, suede or waterproof fabric. They are worn over the top of jodhpurs and provide extra protection and grip for the legs.

Chaps are ideal worn over jeans and boots and will protect you from saddle sores.

High visibility is important when riding on roads. Messages on roadside signs can help to alert drivers.

Tops

For general riding, a shirt such as a T-shirt or sweatshirt is perfectly suitable. When riding out on a trail or hacking on roads, it is advisable to wear fluorescent clothing or bright colors to improve your visibility. For cooler weather, vests are a popular option for many riders. Vests provide more freedom for arms and shoulders and lend themselves to layering for warmth.

Boots

Boots are probably the next most important purchase after your hat. Jodhpur boots and full-length riding boots are the best footwear option for riding. They are designed with a low heel to prevent the foot from sliding through the stirrup iron. Many different styles of boots are available, so it is important to choose a boot that is comfortable, affordable, and suitable for the riding you do. In Western riding, the cowboy boot is still very much the favorite and offers safety and practicality with style.

Undergarments

Undergarments especially designed for sporting activities can make your riding more comfortable. Saddlery shops often carry a selection of bras and underwear suitable for riding. Sports shops specializing in jogging and running clothes are also good places to find comfortable undergarments.

A rider dressed to compete: Competition clothing will vary according to the type of competition you are taking part in.

WHAT NOT TO WEAR

As with so many sports, it is important to look and feel good when riding, but some essential rules need to be observed.

Hat safety

Never ride without the protection of a riding hat. Baseball caps or fabric hats do not provide any protection. Accidents can happen in a split second and a hat could make the difference between walking away with a few cuts and bruises and not walking away at all. In addition, hats should be worn with the chin strap correctly adjusted and done up. In many countries, hard hats are enforced at all competitions.

Footwear

There are many options for riding footwear on the market these days. It is essential, whether riding Western or English style, that you wear a boot with a small heel, as this will prevent your foot slipping through the stirrup and possibly your being dragged

HINT

Think sense, not fashion, when working with horses.

in the event of an accident. Running shoes and most rubber boots should not be used for riding because they lack an adequate heel. Many hiking and winter boots are also unsuitable as the tread on the sole is often too heavy and may jam the foot in the stirrup during a fall.

Outer clothing

You should always wear clothes that fit you well. Jodhpurs or jeans are suitable because they offer a close fit, which allows you greater freedom of movement in the saddle and protects the inner calf from the stirrup leathers. Loose-fitting pants are not suitable because they are liable to become caught in the leathers and affect your position; they may also wrinkle up and cause the skin to chafe. Jackets should always be done up securely to prevent them from flapping. Horses can be easily frightened and if your horse is startled by the sudden movement of your coat, it may bolt to get away from what is perceived as danger.

Accessories

It can be tempting when out riding to take a knapsack along for your belongings. Many horses are calm enough for you to do this and it is totally safe, but consider what you might be carrying. Do not carry sharp objects; if you fall, these may injure your back and cause severe damage. Also be aware of any noise made by the contents and try to keep this to a minimum. Western saddles have attachments for ropes and saddlebags and are designed to carry more than just the rider.

In addition, avoid wearing jewelry when handling or riding horses—very nasty injuries can be caused if rings, earrings or noserings get caught.

This looks like a lot of fun but a fall could result in **severe head injuries.**

Bracelets, earrings, necklaces and rings can easily get caught. **Always tie up long hair** to prevent it catching. **Loose clothes and running shoes** are not very practical.

While it is recommended to carry a cell phone when riding, remember that not all horses understand some of the less "classic" ringtone sounds, so choose your tune carefully if working with youngsters.

HINT

Running shoes can slip right through the stirrup and become stuck.

RIDING HATS

The classic riding hat offers protection with smartness for hacking and competing.

The head is the most vulnerable part of the rider, so the most important item of equestrian riding wear is the riding hat. The riding hat provides essential protection for the rider's head should they fall or be kicked. In some cases, it is also wise to wear a riding hat while handling horses, especially youngsters. When wearing your riding hat, always have the strap adjusted correctly and fastened for maximum protection.

When buying a hat, make sure it conforms to the current safety standards of the American Society for Testing and Materials (ASTM). It is important that any riding hat fits securely but comfortably. The circumference of the head just above the ears should be measured to establish the size of riding hat needed. Local riding equipment stores often have qualified hat fitters who can help you find a suitable hat.

Avoid buying second-hand riding hats; even if the hat looks intact, it can be difficult to tell if it has been subject to a fall or kick that would diminish the protection it offers.

You should buy a new riding hat if your hat has sustained an impact such as a bad fall, if you bang your head, or if you drop it badly—the damage may not be visible on the outside of the helmet, but its protection will be reduced. It is also advisable to replace your hat if it becomes too tight, too loose or too old.

There are three basic types of horse riding hats:

- *Classic riding hat, or hunt cap.* This is a traditional velvet riding hat (*see opposite page*) with a hard peak, usually available in black, brown or navy.

- *Skull cap or jockey cap.* This riding hat was traditionally worn by jockeys but is now a popular riding hat among leisure riders and competitors in other equestrian sports. This hat has no peak, but peaked covers, known as silks, can be placed over the top of the hat. The silk covers are available in velvet to give the appearance of a classic riding hat, and brightly colored material to give the appearance of a jockey cap. There are also novelty silks with eyes, ears, etc., which are popular with young children.

- *Endurance skull protector.* This riding hat looks similar to a bicycle helmet. It is extremely lightweight and ventilated for comfort in warm weather.

Riding hat with vent

Popular with jockeys and event riders, the **skull cap** (above) offers advanced protection from a fall, while the **soft peak** (right) prevents injury to the face.

Endurance riders spend many hours in the saddle, so a hat must provide them with **good ventilation** as well as safety.

BODY PROTECTORS

A body protector should fit well—sitting at shoulder width—for maximum protection.

Body or back protectors, as the name suggests, are designed to give protection to the back and chest area of the rider should he or she fall or be kicked or trodden on during a fall. Protectors are foam-filled vest-type garments worn over riding clothes and under a jacket. They consist of separate front and back panels fastened with Velcro fittings over the shoulders and on each side to ensure a tight fit.

Any body protector must be adjusted to fit securely and reasonably tightly around the body with no red Velcro exposed on the fastenings so they do not move while riding.

Although the body protector may seem stiff and uncomfortable at first, the foam molds itself to the rider's body shape over time to become more comfortable.

There are three categories of body protector, indicated by the color of the label, offering differing levels of protection:

- *Level 1: Black label.* Offers the lowest level of protection and is only considered appropriate for licensed jockeys.
- *Level 2: Brown label.* Offers medium protection and is suitable for most low-risk general riding—which excludes riding on roads or other hard surfaces, riding

Ensure that the front **Velcro fastening** is done up properly for maximum comfort and safety.

over jumps, and riding young or excitable horses.

- *Level 3: Purple label.* Offers the most protection and is appropriate for normal horse riding, competitive horse riding and working with horses.

Injuries cannot be entirely prevented by wearing a body protector but a body protector can reduce the severity of an injury.

Body protectors should be replaced at least every three to four years as the foam padding may start to degrade. When buying a new body protector make sure that it conforms to the current national safety standard. Avoid buying a second-hand body protector as the protection it offers can be reduced if it has been subject to a fall or kick, even if it looks intact.

Some body protectors include protective shoulder pads, or they may be available as an optional extra, offering protection to the rider's shoulders. Many manufacturers will supply custom-fitted body protectors, and some women may find that a larger front panel to back panel is needed to give a more comfortable fit.

BASIC RIDER FITNESS

Jumping requires good muscle tone in the legs.

Being fit is essential for any sport—and riding is no exception. You need to be fit enough for the level of riding you are doing in order to avoid injury and stiffness and to stay balanced and in a good position.

General posture
A good, upright posture on or off a horse is essential and can be gained from flexibility and strength. Good posture allows for the correct use of the muscles when riding. In addition, the ribcage is lifted and the shoulders are relaxed, which aids more effective lung performance.

Basic warmup exercises
Before starting any stretching exercises, take a 10-minute brisk walk to loosen and warm up the muscles. Gradually increase the speed of your walk, but not so much as to make you feel out of breath. If necessary, take water with you on the walk as fluid is essential when exercising.

Stretching exercises
Riding demands a lot of work from the rider's legs. There are many exercises that can help develop the correct leg muscles. The stretches shown on the right are some useful ones. Try these after completing your warmup routine.

HINT
Exercises prior to working or riding not only aid fitness but provide a sense of well-being that will be transferred to your horse.

Stranding stretch for back of the thigh (hamstring): Find a fence that is strong enough to lean on. Place one foot on the lower rung and, while keeping that leg straight, lean forward. You should feel the pull on the hamstring muscles quite quickly. Be careful not to overdo this stretch and ensure that the supporting leg is bent slightly at the knee.

Standing stretch for front of the thigh (quadriceps): Grasp hold of the front of one ankle, keep the back straight and the knees level, and raise the foot. Push the hips forward—this will mean that the heel will not go right to the buttocks. Feel the stretch in the muscles in the front of the thigh. If you need support, use a wall, door or back of a chair.

Standing stretch for the inner thighs (adducters): Keeping the chest lifted, lean forward and support yourself on the thigh of the bent knee. Extend the other leg out to the side until the stretch is felt along the inner thigh. Keep the foot of the extended leg flat on the floor.

Standing stretch for calf: Stand with feet together, then take a large step forward. Bending the knee of the forward leg will enable you to feel the calf muscles stretch in the straight leg. Prevent damage by keeping your weight forward on the front leg.

MOUNTING

The first skill you need to learn in order to ride a horse is how to mount. There are three ways of getting on a horse: from the ground; using a mounting block; having a "leg up."

Before mounting
First of all, check that the girth is sufficiently tight—if too loose, the saddle will slip to one side during mounting. Pull down the stirrups and check they are at approximately the correct length. To do this:

- Stand facing the saddle.
- Place the knuckles of the right hand on the stirrup bar.
- Adjust the leathers so that the stirrup iron reaches into your armpit.

HAVING A "LEG UP"

This method needs an assistant and requires some co-ordination between the two of you.

- Stand facing the horse on its nearside with the reins in your left hand and your assistant standing behind you.
- Lift your left lower leg backward from the knee.
- Your assistant should take hold of your left leg by placing one hand just below the knee and the other above the ankle.
- On an agreed signal—such as one, two, three, lift!—you spring upward; your assistant helps by also pushing you upward.
- As per mounting from the ground, swing your right leg over the horse's back, land gently in the saddle, and place your feet in the stirrups.

USING A MOUNTING BLOCK

It is always preferable to use a mounting block rather than mounting from the ground. This method is easier for the rider, puts less strain on the horse and decreases the chances of the saddle slipping to one side.

- Stand the horse with its nearside close to the mounting block.
- Stand on the mounting block and proceed the same as for mounting from the ground.

Mounting blocks are an easier way of getting on your horse.

Co-ordination between you and your assistant is essential for **a leg up** to be successful.

MOUNTING FROM THE GROUND

It is important that your horse stands still for this procedure. Ask someone to hold the horse if this is a problem.

1 Stand on the horse's left or nearside. Hold the reins in the left hand tightly enough to prevent the horse or pony from moving off during mounting but not so tight that it walks backward or is jabbed in the mouth. Place the left hand on the pommel (front arch) of the saddle. Turn to face the rear of the horse. With your right hand, take the stirrup iron and turn it clockwise.

2 Raise your left leg and place your foot into the stirrup until the ball of your foot rests on the bottom of the stirrup.

3 Place your right hand over the back of the saddle (cantle), and with a small push, spring lightly up. Straighten your left leg and swing your right leg over the back of the horse, remembering to move your right hand forward as you do so, and gently sit in the saddle. Be careful not to kick the horse's quarters as you swing your leg over its back.

4 Place your right foot in the stirrup. Check that the stirrups are the correct length and are also of equal length on both sides.

5 Check the girth is still tight enough— if you can easily run your fingers flat between the girth and the horse's belly, then it will need adjusting.

6 Take up the reins in each hand and you are ready to go.

It is very useful to be able to mount from the nearside (left) and the offside (right) of your horse.

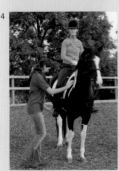

DISMOUNTING

HINT

As with mounting, it is very useful to be able to dismount from either side of your horse.

 is good for horse and rider.

A swift, clean dismount is good for horse and rider.

The dismount

- Bring your horse to a halt—be sure that it is standing obediently and does not move off.
- Always check that you have given yourself a clear, level space on which to dismount.
- Remove both feet from the stirrups.
- Put the reins in your left hand and rest your hand on the horse's neck in front of the withers.
- Put your right hand on the pommel (front) of the saddle.
- In one flowing movement, lean foward, lift your right leg, and swing it over the horse's hindquarters. Be careful not to kick the horse in the process.
- Slide down to the ground, remembering to land on your toes and bend your knees.

After dismounting

Run up each stirrup iron by sliding the iron up the back part of the leather and pássing the folded bottom end of the leather through the center of the iron so that it falls behind it. This prevents the stirrup iron from falling and knocking against the horse. Also remember to reward your horse by loosening the girth by one or two holes.

Once dismounted, run up stirrups and take full control of your horse.

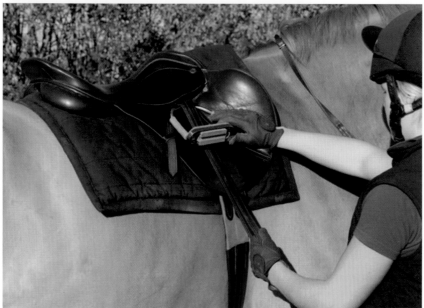

BASIC ENGLISH SEAT

A correctly aligned rider.

Understanding and developing the right seat is crucial to getting the most from your riding. The right seat enables the rider to apply the aids correctly, maintain balance, ride with maximum efficiency and avoid straining muscles.

Correct alignment

When in the saddle, you should be aligned so that a straight line could be drawn that would pass through your ear, shoulder, hip and heel. A correctly aligned rider would land on their feet if their horse were taken out from underneath them by magic.

The seatbones

Your weight should be evenly distributed on both seatbones in the saddle. If you are unsure where your seatbones are, try sitting upright on a hard chair as this will help you locate them.

The upper body

The upper body should "stack" over the top of the seatbones so that you give the impression of sitting tall, straight and relaxed. Do not stiffen your back to achieve this.

A rider needs to develop the right amount of tone in their muscles so that they can maintain a good position without using tension and without being so relaxed that they are easily unbalanced by the horse's movement.

A good position allows the rider to move easily with the horse when in motion.

Holding the reins correctly.

- Your head should be held upright and straight to allow you to look up and through your horse's ears. Looking down stiffens the spine and causes your horse to feel like it is carrying a heavier load.
- Your shoulders should be square, soft and allowed to drop downward.
- Your back should be straight with no stiffness.

The lower body

- Your legs should follow the contour of the horse's body and the saddle. The knees and toes should point forward and the thighs rest against the saddle.
- To gauge the correct length for the stirrups: Sit with your feet out of the stirrups, with your legs hanging gently around the horse, then bump your foot against the stirrup iron. If the stirrup tread touches your ankle bone, the stirrups are the correct length.
- The widest part of your foot should lightly rest on the bar of the stirrup iron. Your heels should be angled, but not pressed down.

The foot rests lightly in the stirrup with just enough pressure to keep the stirrup in place.

Holding the reins

- Pick up the reins in each hand. The rein from the horse's bit should pass between your little finger and your ring finger, lie across the palm of the hand, and the buckle or loose end should pass over the index finger with your thumb on top.
- As you hold the reins, let your arms hang at your sides, with your elbows close to but not touching your body. Hold your hands slightly below your navel, about 6–7 in (15–18 cm) apart.

COMMON PROBLEMS

Developing a good position in the saddle can take time, and a range of common problems often need to be overcome by the novice rider. A rider who is unfit or has yet to develop the correct muscles for riding will find it difficult to maintain the right position.

Daily posture
The way we use our bodies when off horse affects the way we can use them when on horse. A rider who spends hours a day slouched in an office chair in front of a computer is likely to slouch in the saddle. The core stability muscles needed to hold the body tall and straight will not be developed, so when these muscles are needed to maintain a correct position in the saddle, the rider will struggle. Instead, the rider may adopt a position that they find physically easier in an attempt to be more comfortable. The following describes some of the common problems found in riding.

Leaning too far back or slouching
A rider who slouches usually leans too far back. Their legs will either lie too far forward or behind the correct position. They often hold on to the reins too tightly to help them balance and so lean heavily on the horse's mouth. Leaning back and throwing your legs forward places the rider's body weight "behind the vertical," which makes it difficult for the horse to balance itself.

Leaning too far forward
A rider who leans too far forward places their body weight "in front of the vertical." This affects the horse's balance as it needs to move its weight forward onto its shoulders to help carry the rider. This can encourage the horse to lean on the reins and makes it easier for the horse to run off. When leaning forward, the rider's legs are often positioned too far back, which makes communication from the leg aids less effective.

Slouching or leaning too far back upsets the horse's balance.

Knee off the saddle

Often because of lack of muscle development, the rider turns out at the hips. This impacts on the whole leg position as it takes the thigh away from the saddle and turns out the knee and toe. This compromises the rider's balance and lessens the effect of the leg aids.

Gripping with the knees

In trot, a rider who is not properly aligned will usually be unbalanced by the increased movement from the horse. A common response is to grip with the knees in order to gain some stability. In fact, this makes the rider more unstable as they will be pushing their weight upward rather than allowing it to drop down. Performing rising trot then becomes much more difficult to do.

Leg position: too far back.

Leg position: too far forward.

Leg position: knee out.

HINT

Find an indoor school that has mirrors or get a friend to take a picture or video of you riding, so you can see how you sit in the saddle.

RIDING WESTERN

Western riding evolved in North America from the need to spend hours, even days, in the saddle working on cattle ranches. Clothing was meant to be comfortable and durable. The saddle was built of strong leather and designed for rider's comfort and the practicalities of the work. Today, Western-style riding includes trail riding, show classes such as pleasure and reining, and competitions such as barrel racing, pole bending and rodeo.

Western saddlery
The Western saddlery is noticeably different from English, especially the saddle. The Western saddle has a prominent front (pommel) with a horn for carrying a rope or for fixing the rope when lassoing cattle,

a deep seat, a high cantle (back), and long stirrup leathers that encourage a straight leg position. A curb-bridle or bitless bridle is used.

Use of the reins
In Western riding, the reins are usually held in one hand only and there is a considerable amount of slack in the reins, which is not seen in the English style. The Western horse is also taught to neck rein—to move left or right depending on the side of the neck that the rider applies pressure with the rein.

Using weight
Most Western riders apply weight instructions differently from English riders. The Western horse is taught to move away

MOUNTING WESTERN STYLE

1
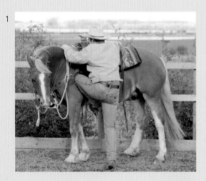

2

3

4

The walk

The jog

from pressure, including weight. This means that the rider's weight is rather on the outside of the horse in a turn-around or a circle, pushing the horse in.

Paces

The quality of the pace is central to the training of the Western horse. The paces are the jog and the lope, which are the trot and the canter with a shorter stride.

- To achieve the jog or lope, place the reins in your less dominant hand, have your legs straight in the saddle, and use your weight to move forward while applying some leg pressure.
- To turn left, apply pressure to the right side while keeping your left leg loose. With the reins in one hand, pull them left across the neck.

- To turn your horse to the right, apply pressure to the outside left leg to encourage the horse to move away from the pressure and with your reins in the one hand, pull them across the neck toward the right.

Western moves

Moves made with a Western horse can be a little different from those taught to English-trained horses. The Western competitive horse is taught to perform a roll-back and reining, where the horse slides to a stop. More advanced moves include the Western spin, where at full speed the horse pivots on the inside hind leg, and the sliding stop, where the horse's hindquarters are lowered to an almost sitting position and the front legs remain loose.

The **lope**

Riding with one hand leaves the other hand free for roping work.

ACHIEVING BALANCE

Balance in the saddle may seem an easy feat to accomplish but, in fact, can be quite difficult to achieve and maintain. Obtaining balance over a horse's constantly changing center of gravity and being able to follow the horse's motion in all paces takes time to learn. Many factors such as poor body use and lack of muscle development play a part in the rider's ability to achieve and maintain balance.

A rider who struggles to achieve balance will take actions to help them stay in the saddle: for example, holding the reins too tight, which in turn pulls the body forward; or not sitting upright in the saddle but slumping, which not only makes for very untidy riding but can increase the weight for the horse to carry.

Off the horse
A useful exercise to help you understand the riding position and get a feel for it without having to think about the horse is as follows:

- Stand with your feet about 2 ft (60 cm) apart and body upright.
- Bend your knees slightly.
- Glance down to check that you can just see your toes, which should be under your knees.
- Look ahead again.
- Check you are standing squarely on both feet with toes pointing forward.
- Your weight should be even on both feet.

You should be able to hold this position for quite a while. When you sit in the saddle, your position should then feel more familiar and easier to maintain.

Working on the instructor's lunge line to improve a rider who is leaning too far back.

Getting closer to the optimum **shoulder–hip–heel alignment**.

Leg pulls stretch and tone leg muscles, helping the leg to lie in the correct position and improving balance.

On the lunge line

Working on the lunge with an instructor or colleague is one of the best ways to improve balance. The instructor will take control of the horse, leaving you free to concentrate on your position and balance. You can perform a wide variety of useful exercises on the lunge.

In the school

The following exercises to help balance and co-ordination can be done by yourself in the school:

- Keep your seat out of the saddle for three strides. In trot, rise for three strides, stay out of the saddle for three strides, then rise again. Alternatively, sit for a few strides (not too many), then rise, then sit again.
- Ride without stirrups. Quit and cross your stirrups and check that you are sitting correctly. Aim to keep your legs and feet in the same position as when you have your stirrups. Start in walk and progress to trot. Try canter if walk and trot work is satisfactory.

Arm exercises on the lunge help improve co-ordination and balance. Your instructor will check whether the leg position alters when other parts of the body are doing different movements.

HINT

Always do any exercises on both reins as you and the horse may find that you favor one side more than the other.

THE AIDS

This rider is communicating with the horse by using gentle **leg pressure**—an aid.

The aids are the physical pressures a rider uses to communicate with the horse. When the horse responds correctly to the pressure, the rider takes the pressure away. This means the horse is rewarded for a correct response.

Aids are not the same as cues. When the horse responds to voice commands or to a click that means trot, he is responding to conditioned cues. Riders communicating via the aids have a full, rich vocabulary with many shades of meaning. In order to take a horse to the upper levels in any sport, a rider needs this larger vocabulary.

There are two types of aids:
- The natural aids, which consist of the legs, the seat or weight aids, and the hands or rein aids.
- The artificial aids, which consist of the whip, spurs and voice. The voice is often used more as a cue than as an aid.

The seat or weight aids
The seat or weight aids can be used to create forward energy and influence direction. Like leg aids, weight aids can be applied bilaterally or unilaterally. To apply the weight aids, the rider drops a little weight into one or both seatbones. When the amount of weight carried on a particular seatbone changes, it is important that the rider's upper body position should not change. Common faults are that the upper body leans and the hip collapses.

The hand or rein aids
These aids are applied to the bit through steady, quiet hands and an elastic wrist guided by loose, flexible elbow and shoulder joints. They should not be used alone but always in conjunction with the leg or seat aids.

THE LEG AIDS

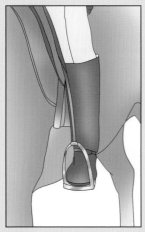

The lower leg lies close to the horse's side but **not in contact** when not in use.

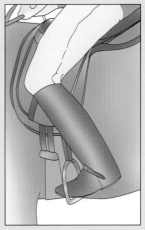

The lower leg pressed against the horse to **apply an aid**.

The leg aids are used to ask the horse to move forward and to indicate direction. The rider applies the leg aid by pressing the inside of the lower leg (with the toe pointing forward, not out) against the horse. Leg aids can be applied with varying degrees of pressure and in different sequences to ask for specific movement.

When both legs actively apply a forward pressure, this is known as a bilateral leg aid: for example, an upward transition to ask the horse to move from halt to walk or from walk to trot. When only one leg is actively pressing and asking the horse to move the hind leg on that side forward, while the other leg just softly holds and steadies, this is known as a unilateral leg aid: for example, asking the horse to turn while in motion or an upward transition into canter.

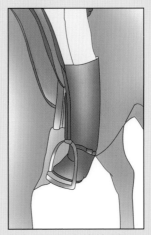

The lower leg applied behind the girth to stop the hindquarters swinging outward on a turn or to apply the aid to canter.

STOPPING AND STARTING

Important early skills to learn when riding are how to ask the horse to halt and how to move forward.

Asking for halt

To ask for a halt, close your fingers around the reins and squeeze backward. As the horse feels the extra pressure on the reins, it should stop. As you gain skill and your aids become more refined, allow your seat to be deeper in the saddle, hold your back, close your legs on the horse slightly, and squeeze the reins. As soon as the horse responds, the instruction should be stopped.

If the horse is reluctant to stop, you will need to apply a stronger aid by pulling backward. This is only advisable for the more experienced rider as, often, pulling too hard and leaning back can make the horse go even

A good, square halt with the horse in balance and its weight evenly carried on all four legs.

faster. Remember a horse's strength is far greater than its rider's.

- Try to feel the rhythm of the horse's strides, squeeze back on the reins, and ease off until the horse halts.
- Avoid a constant "dead" pull on the reins as this will encourage the horse to lean more and set itself against the bit. This will make halting more difficult to achieve as the horse will be fighting against your instruction.
- Do not jerk or jab on the reins as this can injure the mouth and upset the horse.
- Aim to make the transition as smooth as possible, which will help to avoid resistance and the process should be relatively quick.
- If the horse has halted correctly, it should have its nose down and so will remain in balance. The horse should be standing more or less square—a leg "in each corner."
- If the horse throws its head up, you may have applied the aids to halt too sharply. If the horse swings or turns, you may be holding the reins unevenly or be giving uneven leg aids.

Asking for walk

- Hold your reins so that you feel a light contact between your hands and the horse's mouth.
- Use both lower legs to squeeze the horse lightly behind the girth area. This should not be a constant squeeze but a quick on-off movement.
- Your leg above the knee should remain still.
- Your hands should follow the movement of your horse's head and neck as they naturally extend to move forward.

Some horses are less willing to move forward than others. If your horse does not begin to walk forward from your aid, increase the power of the squeeze with your lower leg according to how they are moving. Stop asking as soon as the horse responds and allow it to walk on.

When a horse tries to avoid the halting, keep applying then releasing the aid. Constant pulling may make the situation worse.

THE WALK

Rider maintaining good posture in the walk.

The walk is traditionally the easiest of the horse's paces to manage, even for the novice rider. Once the horse has moved forward from halt, you should be able to identify the rhythm of the walk. As the horse places a hind leg on the ground, the hindquarters on that side lowers, which will automatically drop your seatbone on that side. As the horse lifts its hind leg and transfers the weight to the other side, your seatbone will be pushed up and forward and the other seatbone is lowered. This motion remains constant for the horse and for the rider.

Riding the walk

- Look forward in the direction you want to go and remain soft and supple.
- Maintain good posture. Make sure you are sitting evenly balanced in the saddle. If you sit with more weight on one side, it will be harder for your horse to understand and perform some of your commands.
- Keep your lower leg quiet unless you are asking the horse to change to a trot or halt. Do not let your feet slide forward or your legs swing. Look downward briefly to check that your toes are not visible.
- Keep your thighs, knees and feet pointing forward. This helps keep your seat secure and makes asking for the next transition easier.
- Even at the walk you should be working to keep a good position.

NEAR HIND

NEAR FORE

The walk is a four-beat pace. The sequence of the footfalls is near hind, near fore, off hind, off fore.

This Western rider is in walk.

- Your hands should maintain a light contact on the reins. As the horse walks, its head will move slightly with each step and you should allow your hands to follow this movement as you hold the reins.

Walk in Western

When neck reining, you are most likely to hold the reins in one hand. This may cause you to carry that shoulder more forward. To keep the correct balance and non-transference of weight, carry the hand that is not holding the reins in a way that keeps your shoulders even. Some riders hold their arm bent at the elbow, across the front of their bodies, and some opt to keep their arms straight.

OFF HIND

OFF FORE

During the walk, the horse always has at least **two feet on the ground** at the same time.

THE TROT

The trot is a two-beat pace, with the horse's legs moving in diagonal pairs separated by a moment of suspension. It can be ridden in rising or sitting trot.

The quality of a horse's trot depends on its conformation. Some are built with good suspension and are able to absorb concussion well through their joints. Such horses give a smooth ride and so their trot is easier for the rider to deal with. Horses with poor suspension can have a jarring trot, which is not as comfortable to ride and makes sitting trot particularly difficult.

Rising trot
The rising trot gives relief to the horse's back by moving the rider's weight off the back muscles. This is particularly necessary on long rides or when riding a young horse that has not developed fully in its back.

Points to note include:
- Your upper body moves upward and forward, rather than in just an upward direction.
- You must maintain a good position and keep your toe under your knee. When the toe is in front of the knee, the rider sits as if in a chair with the feet forward and backside pushed to the back of the saddle. The rider then has to lever her- or himself up and down out of the saddle in order to rise to the trot.

To perform rising trot:
- Ask for an upward transition in walk by squeezing with your lower leg.
- Sit for a few strides to establish the rhythm.
- Lift out of the saddle, bringing your upper body slightly forward from your hips and letting your hips swing slightly forward toward the pommel (front arch of the saddle).
- With the next stride, lower your seat lightly back into the saddle, keeping your shoulders slightly forward of the rest of your body.
- Repeat the process for each stride.

Think of allowing your pelvis to swing forward and back, as if making an arc shape. By doing this, the horse's movement will take you, instead of you having to heave

In rising trot, it is important that the rider is on the correct diagonal. On the left rein, the rider should sit in the saddle when the horse's left hind leg and right foreleg (the left diagonal) are forward. This helps the horse to balance the rider's weight more easily.

Working on the lunge without stirrups can help to improve your sitting trot.

yourself out of the saddle, against the horse's movement, which is much more effort for both of you.

If you find yourself getting out of rhythm with the horse, return to either sitting trot or walk before returning to rising trot again.

Sitting trot

In trot, the horse's back moves up and down, so for sitting the rider needs to be able to absorb this movement to avoid being thrown up and down. If you ride stiffly, you will bounce up and down; if you ride too relaxed, you will wobble around. To remain softly in the saddle, you need to be able to use your lower back, abdominal muscles and pelvis to match the movement of the horse's back. It helps to start on a lunge line with stirrups and leathers removed, particularly if you are a novice.

To perform sitting trot:

- Once mounted, place your palms on the pommel and push yourself up out of the saddle, at the same time spreading your legs in a wide "V."
- Lower your seat back into the saddle and feel the difference in your seat.
- As the horse trots, your back should flex to emphasize the natural slight hollow in your lower back. Your pelvis should rock forward onto the front edge of your seatbones but it is important that the upper body remains still.
- The pelvis should then return to the upright position, so that the back is flattened again.
- At first aim for only a few strides. Always stop with the first bounce and reposition. Gradually add more strides. This will be easier on both you and the horse.
- Once you begin to bump with every stride your horse's back will stiffen in self-defense and the bouncing just gets worse.

It can be useful to practice the movement of the sitting trot off horse. Sit on a stool and flex your back in, then flatten it—feel how your seatbones rock forward and backward, acting as a pivot point.

In the two-beat pace of the trot, the footfall sequence is near hind and off fore together (left diagonal), off hind and near fore together (right diagonal).

LEFT DIAGONAL

RIGHT DIAGONAL

THE CANTER

Right rein canter on the correct leg. To check for the correct lead when riding canter, look for inside foreleg being clearly in front of the outside.

Once you feel comfortable in trot, the next step is canter or, if riding Western, lope. It is useful to start work on canter on the lunge line; your instructor can be in control of the horse while you concentrate on your seat.

To perform canter
- Establish a good, rhythmic trot.
- Sit for a few strides.
- To ask for canter, slide your outside leg back slightly to lie just behind the girth, while maintaining the inside leg position against the girth, then squeeze with both lower legs. Using your legs in this position encourages your horse to begin the canter on the correct lead—that is, it uses its outside hind leg to start the canter—and to bend around your inside leg.
- You should feel your horse lift his shoulders and push with its hindquarters.
- Depending on how willing your horse is to stay in canter, you may need to squeeze with your inside leg occasionally to maintain the forward motion.

- Keep your reins at a length where you can maintain a gentle but steady contact with the bit as the horse lifts its head. Allow your hands to follow the movement of the horse's head and neck. Western riders will not ride with a contact but follow the movement without pulling on the reins.
- As in the sitting trot, allow your pelvis and lower back to follow the rocking motion of the horse. By doing this, your shoulders and upper back should be able to remain upright and not sway.
- To return to trot, bring your outside leg forward to its position at the girth, resist the forward motion of the horse's head by squeezing the outside rein then releasing the pressure. If the horse does not trot immediately, continue to squeeze and release on the reins until it trots.
- Once in trot, the horse should continue to move forward actively. If it continues to slow down, you will need to apply the leg aids to keep the horse going.

A poor position in canter. Following the horse's movement with your pelvis and lower back will allow you to maintain a good position.

The correct position of the outside leg when preparing for canter.

Checking the correct lead

- Once you have established canter, you should check that your horse is on the correct lead. When you first learn canter, it will be easier to do this by using your peripheral vision to look down at the shoulder and foreleg—the inside foreleg should lead in front of the outside foreleg. Be careful not to tip your head down to look as this will move you out of the correct position. As you become more experienced, you will be able to feel the motion of the leading foreleg pulling your hip slightly forward.
- If your horse starts canter using the wrong leg, you should come back to trot again and then attempt to canter on the correct leg.

NEAR HIND   OFF HIND & NEAR FORE   OFF FORE

Canter is a three-beat pace. Footfall sequence for canter: on the right rein—near hind, off hind and near fore together, off fore; on the left rein—off hind, near hind and off fore together, near fore.

THE GALLOP

Preparing to gallop—gathering the reins and holding on to the mane.

Asking to move up to gallop.

The gallop is an exhilarating feeling but should not be attempted until you have sufficient experience, skill and confidence. It is worth checking whether your horse can gallop, as not all are adept at this level of speed.

Never gallop in a confined space but, if possible, pick a field that has good wide grass tracks around the outside. If you have not ridden down the track before, take the time to walk your horse along it and check for any ruts or holes. If your horse puts its foot into one of these at speed, it is very likely to fall, resulting in possible damage and injury to both of you.

It is also useful to know at what point you will need to start thinking about asking for a down transition to canter. By knowing your track, you will be able to do this with confidence. If your horse has a tendency to be a little strong, never leave this to the last minute.

Performing the gallop

- Establish a good canter.
- Raise your seat slightly out of the saddle and stand in your stirrups.
- Shorten your reins and lean forward. If necessary, hold your horse's mane to help you keep your balance and prevent you from jabbing it in the mouth.
- Squeeze with your lower legs to ask the horse to move faster.
- While allowing your body to move with your horse's stride, push your weight forward to encourage your horse to "go on."
- Keep your body weight low and as horizontal as possible while remaining standing in the stirrups.
- To return to canter, start to squeeze back and release on the reins, lower your seat back into the saddle, and slowly start to sit upright and adopt the canter position. If the horse resists, continue to apply slightly stronger aid with the reins while squeezing gently with your legs.

Western horse and rider in full gallop.

TURNING AND CIRCLES

Horse demonstrating **correct bend for circle**.

Turning and circles are essential training for any horse and rider to improve suppleness and balance. Top-level dressage riders perform many routines that may look simple but, in practice, can be much harder than they seem.

If your horse is not terribly fit, then using the muscles to perform correct turns and circles can be extremely hard work, so build up this work gradually to avoid the risk of injury.

The perfect turn and circle

To achieve a perfect turn or circle, the horse should bend from his poll through his body to his tail. The inside hind leg should step under the hindquarters and follow the track of the inside front leg.

If possible, ride your turns and circles on a riding area or indoor school until you are familiar with the process. The sides of the school will help you to gauge the shape of the circle more accurately.

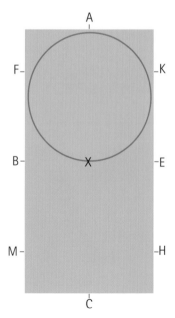

Area for turning in the **65 ft (20 m) circle**.

The 65 ft (20 m) circle

- In walk, leave the track at A or C and aim to just touch the track on the long side of the arena to complete the first quarter of the circle.
- Carry on turning so that you create a "half moon" to reach the center point of the school at X.
- The third quarter of the circle should also just touch the opposite long side.
- Then continue on around to rejoin the track where you started.
- Once you have a feel for the shape of the circle, try performing it at E or B, which can be a little more difficult to gauge.

The aids for turning

- The inside hand squeezes and releases the rein to encourage the horse to bend its head in the direction of the turn.
- The outside hand controls the pace and allows the horse's head to bend without checking.
- The inside leg remains on the girth to encourage the horse to bend around it.
- The outside leg moves behind the girth to prevent the hindquarters from moving out.

As you become more competent and your horse becomes fitter, turns and circles can be performed in canter and the circles can become smaller.

Neck reining

Neck reining is a useful skill to acquire whether you ride English or Western style. It leaves one hand free to open gates, use a whip or carry an object.

- Hold both reins in one hand.
- Traditionally, Western riders hold the reins in their non-dominant hand, leaving their dominant (usually right) hand free for work such as handling a rope or opening a gate.
- Your hand should be centered a few inches in front of your body.
- To turn right, lift your hand slightly and move it right to lay the right rein on the right side of the horse's neck—no pressure should be applied to the bit.
- As you lay the rein on the horse's neck, apply pressure with the left leg to encourage the horse to bend around that leg.
- When the turn is complete, release the pressure and return your hand to center.

Turning Western style

KEEPING CONTROL

An event rider falling into water.

No one wants to ride in fear but horses can be unpredictable creatures—if you ride you are likely to fall at some time. Jumping sports increase the risk, as does increased speed. When frightened or startled, even the most dependable horse can put a rider in potential danger.

How to avoid a fall

- Ride a horse that matches your level of skill and experience.
- Stay in control and remain focused.
- Ride with awareness, especially when out on a hack.
- When riding a horse or in a saddle that does not belong to you, check the equipment before getting on and adjust the stirrups before setting off.
- Check that your girth or cinch is adequately tightened so that the saddle does not slip. Remember to re-check the girth once you have been riding for a few minutes.

In the event of a fall
- Always wear a body protector for show-jumping or cross-country. It will help to avoid serious injuries but may not stop them entirely.
- Ensure your feet are out of the stirrups—using correct footwear and stirrups will prevent you from getting a foot caught.
- Use the horse's neck to push yourself away from him and try to hit the ground as if rolling into a ball.
- Keep your arms tucked in to prevent them getting broken or trodden on by your horse.
- If you hit the ground particularly hard but are clear of the horse, wait a few moments and regain your breath before getting up.
- If the fall is at a walk, possibly because the horse trips, try to hold on to the reins.

- If the fall is at any speed, do not try to hold on to the reins—this could pull the horse on to you or cause it to drag you.

After a fall
- Give yourself a few seconds to get your breath back.
- Quickly assess both yourself and your horse.
- Depending on the type of fall, you may need to inspect your horse more thoroughly and run your hands down its legs to check for possible injury.
- If there is no apparent damage to either of you, then remount. This will reassure yourself, your horse and any riding companions.
- Being stoic about pain might seem valiant, but if you have broken a bone, do not attempt to ride as you could worsen the injury.

If your horse should rear up, don't panic! Stay calm, retain balance and attempt to bring the horse back under control.

BASIC JUMPING

Instructor using the length of her stride to measure the distance between poles.

Jumping is great fun for both horse and rider and demonstrates great athletic ability.

Teaching the rider or horse to learn how to jump should be done in gradual stages. If either are pushed too much too soon, the rider is likely to become frightened and the horse will lose confidence and start to refuse.

Pole and gridwork enables a horse to start judging distances and is particularly useful for helping young horses to learn balance and rhythm. If you are not familiar with setting out gridwork, ask an experienced rider to help you or have a lesson with an instructor.

A gridwork routine

- Place three or four poles at an equal distance apart down one of the long sides of a school.
- Place a single pole on the opposite side of the school.

- Walk over the single pole. The first time you do this, the horse, especially if young, may want to look at the pole. Allow the horse to lower its head while encouraging it to keep moving forward with your leg aids.
- Walk down the line of three poles.
- If this is successful, go into trot and proceed over the single pole once again.
- Now trot down the line of poles. On approaching this line, do not allow the horse to study the poles too much but encourage it to go forward actively.
- Once you and your horse are confident over the poles, ask an assistant to make a small cross-pole jump with the last two poles.
- In trot, practice your approach and striding into this.

Poles laid out at equal distances apart.

Make sure that you practice these poles on both reins as it is important that both horse and rider develop suppleness in both directions.

Once you have a small grid of poles set up, place more poles around the school with a selection of cross poles at the end of the grid. Work this into a small course, maintaining trot throughout.

Trotting over poles in jumping position.

Using gridwork to help with problems

If your horse rushes its jumps, gridwork is an excellent way to encourage the horse to slow down as it approaches the jump.

- Place three trotting poles equal distances apart followed by a small jump, possibly at about 2 ft (60 cm).
- Approach the jump in trot. If the horse starts to rush, do not interfere with its mouth by pulling on the reins as the poles will act as a natural break.
- After you have gone over the last element, continue in canter for two strides before returning back to trot.

Trotting over poles to a small cross-pole jump.

BOUNCE STRIDES

Bounce strides

A bounce stride is used for jumping two fences where the distance between the fences does not allow the horse to take a stride between them. The horse lands over the first jump and as soon as the back legs touch the ground, the front legs take off for the second jump.

Bounce strides are useful for developing the athleticism and agility of a horse but can be both mentally and physically demanding. Avoid practicing bounce strides for more than 20 minutes in one lesson.

- Place a set of four poles at equal distance apart and trot down the line.
- Change the middle two poles into cross-poles. Adjust the distance so that it allows for a bounce stride in between the two cross-poles and two full strides from the first pole and to the last pole.

Judging distances

An experienced rider will be able to judge distances and to alter their horse's stride accordingly so that they reach a fence at the right point for takeoff.

Related distances refers to jumps that are related to each other by between three and five non-jumping strides. They can either be in a straight line or at an angle. When jumping a course, related distances allow the horse and rider to continue in a balanced style and to maintain a rhythmical canter into and away from a fence.

- Set out some poles with a distance of three, four or five non-jumping strides between them.
- Practice shortening your stride so that you are able to ride five strides in a four-stride distance and six strides in a five-stride distance.
- Once you have achieved this over poles, replace the poles with small cross-pole jumps.

Rider approaching first jump from poles.

Increasing the height

Once you are confident with cross-poles, start to introduce some higher uprights and spreads. With the change in height of the fence, the horse may jump short or long. In this case, you need to work on either lengthening or shortening your stride to reach the next fence on the right stride.

- If you land short over a jump, kick on and ask the horse to lengthen its stride.
- If you land long, gather up your reins and bring the horse back to a shorter stride.

Attempting the **second jump**

Approximate **distances** for combination fences with approach in trot (1) and canter (2).

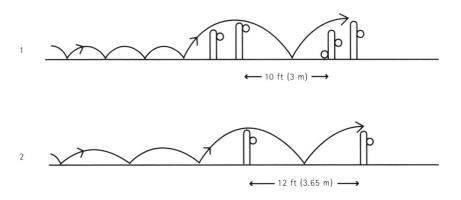

1 ←— 10 ft (3 m) —→

2 ←— 12 ft (3.65 m) —→

THE RIGHT INSTRUCTOR

Choosing the right instructor is important to ensure that you **get the most from your lessons** and that you enjoy them.

Before you start your search for an instructor, consider what your potential aim is. Do you want to compete? If so, what discipline interests you? Dressage, cross-country, show-jumping? Do you just want to become a proficient rider so that you can ride out with friends or on a holiday?

The freelance instructor

If you have your own horse and wish to have lessons to improve your skill in a certain area, then a freelance instructor may be able to help you.

- Word of mouth is the best way, so ask other riders if they can recommend someone.
- Check some of the many websites and magazines that advertise instructors.
- Take the time to talk to a potential instructor and find out about their experience and successes.

- Try to see an instructor teaching others—this may help you decide whether they will suit you or not.
- Be clear about your riding goals. This will not only help you evaluate the suitability of different riding instructors but will also help the instructor understand your expectations.
- Check what level of instruction they offer—some instructors specialize with riders at certain levels, such as beginners or advanced.
- If you want to work in a particular discipline, choose an instructor with a successful background in that sport. They will have a good understanding of the discipline and should know how to develop and challenge their students to enable them to be competitive in that sphere.

The riding school

If you are a beginner, start by looking in your local telephone directory for riding schools in your area. Word of mouth is also an excellent way, so ask riding friends for recommendations. When you are learning to ride, it is not always easy to know how to differentiate between good and bad schools. Before riding at a school, it is useful to book a visit to check their facilities.

- Is the school clean and relatively tidy?
- Is it licensed and does it have adequate insurance?
- Are the instructors adequately qualified?

- Is the school approved by any societies?
- Do they have clear drills in the event of accidents or emergencies?
- Is anyone trained in first aid?
- Do their hats meet the right safety standards?
- Can they provide indoor as well as outdoor lessons? Riding in winter can be extremely cold for both horse and rider.
- Do the horses look healthy, well kept and well mannered?
- Do they have a range of horses that can match your height, weight and skill level?

A good riding school should be able to cater to a range of clients.

A good instructor takes pride in helping their pupils to progress, so tell your instructor exactly what you want from your lessons at the start.

HINT

Make sure that your riding instructor has adequate insurance.

LESSONS

Whether you are having lessons purely to learn to improve your riding technique or you want to excel in a certain discipline, it is always best to be well prepared for lessons in order to get the most out of your time and money.

Lessons at a riding school
- Be on time.
- Check which horse you are riding.
- If you are allowed to tack up, leave plenty of time to do this properly and safely.
- If you are borrowing a hat from your riding school, make sure you get the right size and adjust the chin strap accordingly.
- When you first get on your horse, ensure that the stirrups are at the correct length and check the girth is adequately tightened.

Lessons with your own instructor
If you have lessons with an instructor, they may need you to travel to them for the lesson. If you have your own facilities, the following suggestions will ensure that you get the most from your lesson:
- Travel tacked up to save time on arrival.
- If you are traveling a long distance, ensure your vehicle has enough fuel for the journey.
- When you arrive and unload your horse, let your trainer know you have arrived.
- Allow yourself up to 10 minutes before your lesson starts to go through your usual warmup routine on the arena. This way both you and your horse are sufficiently ready for the physical demands of the lesson.

Lessons at a riding school help you understand different aspects of horse care, such as **getting your horse ready to ride**.

Warm up before your lesson starts to **make the most of your time** with your instructor.

- Before you start your lesson, check the girth.
- If you intend to jump, make sure you have the horse's boots and your back protector on hand.
- Make sure that you practice the work from your lesson before your next session with your instructor. This will help your skills become established and your instructor will be able to help your riding develop more each lesson.

Unless you have a special arrangement, instructors should be paid at the end of each lesson, so be sure to have the right amount of money with you.

Make sure that your stirrups are the right length for you and the girth has been adequately tightened before your lesson begins.

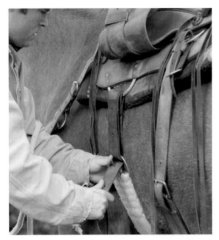

Cinch on Western saddle

Cinch

This is a strap 3 to 4 in (7–10 cm) wide that holds the Western saddle in place on the back of the horse and prevents it from slipping sideways and, to some extent, forward or backward. It also connects the two sides of the saddle underneath the horse's belly.

Changing the rein

When riding in a clockwise direction around a school, you are on the right rein; when riding counterclockwise, you are on the left rein. "Changing the rein" means changing from the right rein to the left rein or vice versa. There are several ways of doing this but a common one is to cross one of the long diagonals—K to M/M to K on the right rein, or F to H/H to F on the left rein.

Diagonal

In trot, the horse moves from one diagonal pair of legs to the other. To be on the correct diagonal in rising trot, the rider sits in the saddle when the inside hind leg and outside foreleg are forward and on the ground.

Disunited

In canter, the horse's sequence of footfall is incorrect—taking one lead with the forelegs and the opposite lead with the hind legs so that the leading foreleg and hind leg appear to be on the same side. Being disunited may arise from of a lack of balance or stiffness in the horse's back.

Drop and cross stirrups

In a lesson, it may be necessary to do some work without stirrups. In this case, the rider should remove their feet from the stirrups, pull the leather's buckle slightly away from the stirrup bar and gently fold the stirrup over the front of the saddle. This should be done with both stirrups, which prevents them from hitting the horse's side when in motion.

Leg aids

Also known as lower aids, this refers to the rider's legs when used to communicate with the horse, such as when producing forward movement, changing direction or asking for halt.

Nearside/offside

The nearside of a horse is its left side; the offside is its right side.

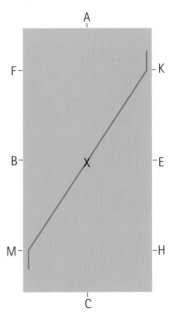

Changing the rein across the long diagonals.

On the bit

A horse "on the bit" takes a light contact on the bit, is responsive to the rider's hands and any slight change the rider may make, carries itself easily and is well balanced.

On the forehand

This describes a horse when it places its weight in front of its center of gravity. This makes the horse unbalanced and it is more difficult to ride.

The 65 ft (20 m) circle

A 65 ft (20 m) circle is used when working in a school and as part of a dressage test. It can be performed in walk, trot or canter. The horse can either leave the outside track at A or C and perform a circle that takes them through the center at X and back around the track, rejoining the outside track at the point at which they left—or leave it at B or E in a 65 ft (20 m) arena.

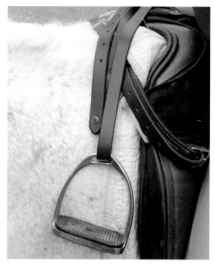

Drop and cross stirrups

On the bit: The horse and rider are communicating well.

PRACTICE DRILLS

Regardless of your preferred discipline, you will need to spend some time on schooling. This is important for both you and your horse in order to develop the balance, suppleness, responsiveness and understanding needed in any sphere of riding.

Ideally, your schooling session should last for between 30 and 45 minutes with adequate warmup and cool-down, but there may be occasions when less time is available to you. If possible, perform the following exercises in a school as this can help make the size and shape of the exercise more accurate; however, many exercises can also be done on a hack. Always ride an exercise on both reins to ensure equal development on both sides of you and your horse.

Circles

Circles test the horse's suppleness and the rider's ability to keep the horse on the aids. Incorrect position or aids will be apparent on a 65 ft (20 m) circle. The horse's body should follow the shape of the circle, so that he stretches the muscles on the outside of the circles and shortens on the inside.

A 65 ft (20 m) circle should be round, not egg- or pear-shaped, or straight lines with rounded edges. This means that, where the circle touches the side of the arena, it should not be ridden along the side for any period of time. Problems include going too deep into the corners of the arena, causing the circle to bulge out so that the horse is not correctly bent on the circle, or overusing the inside rein so that the horse bends its neck into the circle but does not bend through the body.

Once you are competent with 65 ft (20 m) circles, you can begin work on 50 and 30 ft (15 and 10 m) circles. These require more bend and more balance from the horse and will highlight problems with the rider such as an uneven seat or poor position.

Figure-eight

As the name suggests, the rider performs a figure in the shape of an 8 in the arena. This

Circle

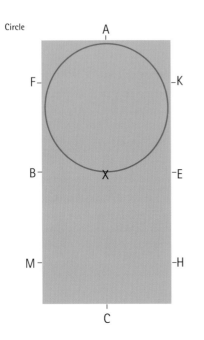

Figure-eight

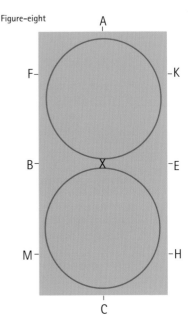

can be used as a means to change direction as well as for schooling.

This figure is usually ridden as the shape of two 65 ft (20 m) circles, rather than having any straight sections to it. You will need to change from one circle to the other at X. Just as you are approaching X you will need to change the direction that the horse is bending and, if in rising trot, to also change your diagonal. Problems will occur at X if your horse is not bending correctly on the first circle—he will find it difficult to change direction, resulting in a poor shape to the circle and loss of balance.

Loops

On the long side of the arena, leave the track at the first marker in a gentle curve aiming to touch the quarter line at 15 ft (5 m) in from the track by the time you reach E or B. Return to the track at the next marker. Change the horse's bend when you reach the quarter line to help your horse return to the track smoothly. Do not leave the track too

late at the first marker or you will run out of space to make the change of bend. Once you are proficient at this exercise, move on to 30 ft (10 m) loops.

Serpentines

This is an S-shaped figure, usually with three or four loops. This suppling exercise requires changes of direction and bend while maintaining rhythm and balance. Aim for a few strides of straightness between each loop and for each loop to be of equal size and shape. Once you have mastered the three-loop serpentine, increase the challenge by riding a four-loop serpentine—each loop will need to be smaller and so will require more bend and balance.

> **HINT**
>
> The more you practice the more you will become familiar with the positioning of the letters in the ring.

Loop

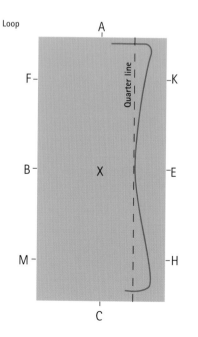

Serpentine

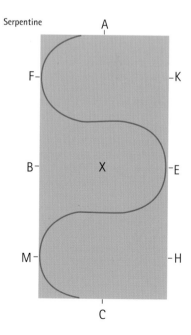

PRACTICE DRILLS

Changing the rein

When working on your schooling, it is useful to know several different ways to change the rein. This can help to add variety to your routines. Some of the usual changes are:

- Down the center line.
- Across the long diagonal.
- Across the short diagonal.
- Center across, from E to B or from B to E.
- Through a half 30 ft (10 m) circle returning to the track.
- Through two half 65 ft (20 m) circles.

Schooling routines

Work out a few programs using the various exercises, changes of rein and transitions. As ever it is important to take the time for both horse and rider to warm up properly before starting on a training routine. Never ignore the need to warm up or you run the risk of losing valuable days because of sprains or strains.

- Warm up in your usual way. In trot, ride a transition from trot to walk and then walk to trot at alternate markers—for example, trot at A, walk at E. Note your leg position for each transition and ensure that the horse does not start to anticipate your intention to change gait.
- At A or C ride a 65 ft (20 m) circle. Note your leg position for the circle and do not allow the horse to fall in on the corner. Change the rein across the long diagonal. Repeat the transition exercise at alternative markers.
- At A or C ride a 65 ft (20 m) circle. Down the next long side ride a 15 ft (5 m) loop. Change the rein across the short diagonal. Down the next long side ride a 15 ft (5 m) loop. As you go down the next long side, prepare for canter at the next corner.
- At E or B ride a 65 ft (20 m) circle.
- Rejoin the track and change the rein across the next long diagonal with a transition down to trot at X.
- At A or C ride a serpentine. As you go down the next long side, prepare for canter at the next corner.

- At E or B ride a 65 ft (20 m) circle. Rejoin the track and change the rein across the next long diagonal with a transition down to trot at X.
- At A or C ride a transition down to walk and allow the horse to walk on a long rein to stretch its neck.
- Walk one full circuit and then, at a suitable point, change the rein and walk another full circuit.

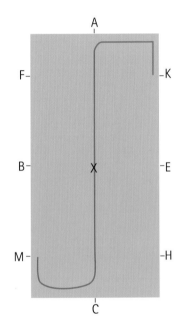

Center line exercise

HINT

Drills can be hard work but try to make sure that you and your horse enjoy them.

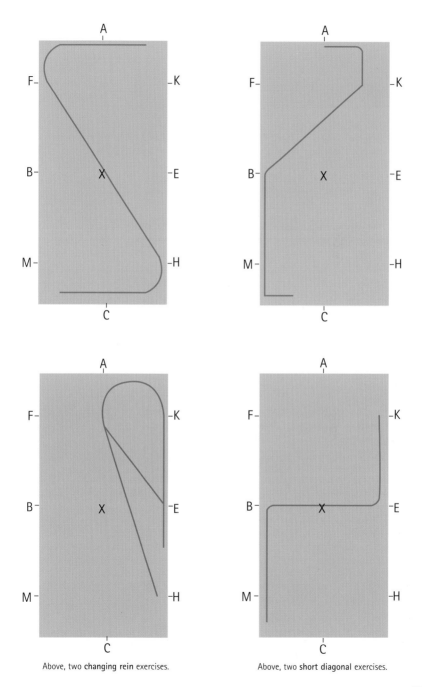

Above, two **changing rein** exercises.

Above, two **short diagonal** exercises.

BASIC NEEDS OF A HORSE

A well-maintained, safe paddock is essential for the well-being of your horse.

Safe environment
A horse must have access to pasture that is free from hazards that could cause injury, such as loose fencing, holes or machinery, and is also free from poisonous plants, such as ragwort and yew. The pasture must be well enclosed with safe fencing on all sides.

Forage and grazing
Because horses eat approximately 2.5 percent of their body weight each day, a constant supply of appropriate forage must be provided in the form of good-quality grazing or hay. As a general rule, the amount of land needed to support a horse is at least one acre per horse, preferably two.

In the wild, horses naturally graze over hundreds of acres, selecting and eating a surprisingly large variety of herbs and minerals to balance their diets. Therefore, the domestic horse must have access to salt and mineral supplements that are available in the form of licks from most feed stores. These can be left in the field for the horse to use at will.

Water
Horses must have access to a supply of fresh, clean water at all times.

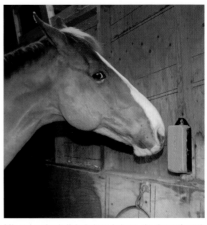

Mineral and salt licks help to balance the domesticated horse's diet.

Shelter
Adequate shelter must be provided from wind and rain in the winter months and from the heat and sun in the summer. A dry, clean area must also be provided for the horse to lie down on.

Monitoring
Horses need regular monitoring, preferably twice a day. They should be checked for evidence of injury or illness by an

As a herd animal, the company of other horses is important for your horse.

experienced person. At the same time, the troughs must be inspected to ensure that clean, adequate water is available and the fences checked for signs of breakage that may enable the horse to escape.

Company
Horses are naturally social animals and it is important that they are allowed to live in company, preferably with other horses, but sheep, goats, or even cattle will suffice. As a herd animal, they like to spend much of their day in the company of other horses, drinking, grazing, grooming and also resting together at the same time.

Understanding
It is very important that people who look after horses understand them. As a breed, they are extremely reactive animals and have a deep-rooted "fight or flight" instinct that has been honed over millions of years. This must be respected and taken into account at all times.

91

THE GRASS-KEPT HORSE

It is essential when **keeping horses at grass** to provide them with a safe and secure environment.

How much grass

Generally, you should provide at least one acre of land per horse as minimum and up to two acres if possible. If horses are turned out all year round, their grazing should be rotated to allow the grass to be rested on one area while they graze another. This also gives you the opportunity to perform some pasture management such as harrowing, fertilizing or removing weeds.

Fencing options

If your land is not bordered by naturally thick hedging, it will be necessary to erect separate fencing. One of the most effective and attractive options is post and rail fencing, but it can be quite expensive. One cheaper alternative is to use rustic poles spanned by tape that can be electrified from a power supply. It is an efficient method of fencing and horses do learn to respect it. If possible, always allow sufficient space for a

vehicle to enter the field—in the case of an emergency or any repair work it can be a great help.

Water

A regular supply of fresh, clean water is absolutely essential. If your land is not supported by a trough fed automatically from the water supply, then you will need to provide a large container that is filled manually. Such containers should be refilled on a daily basis and cleaned out regularly. Particular attention should be paid during the summer months when horses require more water and during periods of frost and snow when ice should be broken at least twice a day.

Shelter

Horses must be provided with some form of shelter. Hedges and trees form a natural shelter. Nowadays, manufactured field

A field shelter will provide good protection from the elements. Make sure your shelter has adequate space to accommodate all the animals turned out.

The water trough must always be filled with fresh water.

shelters are often erected in fields. They offer horses the opportunity to get away from wind, driving rain and snow in the winter and also offer protection from flies and the heat of the day in the summer. A field shelter should be three-sided and built to a size that easily accommodates all the horses that may be turned out together at any one time.

FEEDING FOR HEALTH

Hay is the main bulk food replacement for grass. Always feed hay that is clean and of good quality.

The rule "feed little and often" should always be applied to horses. They are designed to be trickle feeders, with small stomachs in relation to body size and need to top up with food regularly. This means a horse has a small amount of food in it at all times and never a lot at once, as it cannot cope with digesting large quantities. This makes it an eating machine, and a horse in the wild will travel miles for food, foraging between 16 and 18 hours a day on a diet consisting mainly of grass with additional vitamins and minerals from other plants as they find them.

For the domesticated horse, the same rules apply. The horse's stomach is very fragile and overfeeding or feeding of poor-quality, unsuitable foods could easily lead to digestive problems such as colic. Feeding a highly palatable and well-balanced diet is a vital part of horse ownership. Smaller grazing areas and stabling mean that the horse will not have access to the wide variety of vitamins and minerals found in the wild, so a suitable replacement must be supplied. Good-quality hay and grass should be available, with increased quantities provided during colder weather when the horse uses a lot of its energy to keep warm. Additional feed is most important during the winter months, as any horse kept without proper nutrition will be more susceptible to disease and infection.

Chaff or chop adds bulk to a horse's feed. It is usually added to concentrates to encourage chewing and help digestion.

Extruded feeds.

Beet pulp is a highly digestible source of energy and roughage. It should always be soaked for 12 hours before being fed to horses. If not adequately soaked, it can swell in the horse's stomach with possibly fatal results.

Extruded feeds and coarse mixes are specially formulated concentrate feeds that provide a standardized, balanced diet. They are available in a range of varieties, from low-energy to competition mixes.

Feeding horses is a complex practice. All horses are different, with varying requirements and workloads, and so need be fed accordingly—the dietary requirements of a riding club horse will not be the same as that of a race or event horse. For many horses, at rest or in light work, a diet of good-quality hay and grass would be perfectly adequate to keep them healthy. However, horses with greater workloads or horses that are older should have part of their bulk food ration replaced by concentrates such as coarse mixes or extruded foods. Concentrates have a higher energy value than forage and are specially formulated to maintain and improve body condition.

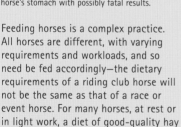

HINT

Never make any sudden change to a horse's diet—introduce new feedstuffs gradually.

HOOFCARE

The hoof

The hoof is the protective outer layer of the horse's foot, consisting of the hard outside wall, and the sole and frog underneath. While it is attached to the delicate bone structure of the foot, the hoof itself contains no blood supply or nerves, which is why it is possible to hammer nails and apply hot iron shoes to it without causing the horse any pain.

Diet for good hoof growth

A well-balanced diet directly reflects on the condition of the hoof. In most horses, a general mix of vitamins, minerals and good-quality forage should be enough to maintain good hoof quality. Some nutrients have been singled out for helping to promote strong hoof development, such as biotin and DL methionine, both of which can be bought as separate supplements from feed stores. There are also many hoof dressings available—some are purely cosmetic and have no effect on development; more useful products are either oil based or contain silicone or wax.

Shoeing

The most important way to care for your horse's feet is to visit a professionally trained farrier. Because all horses use their bodies

A **well-shod** hoof.

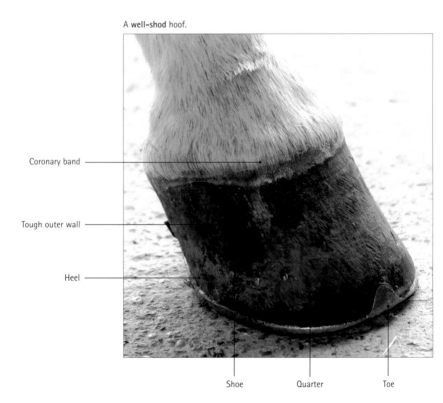

Coronary band

Tough outer wall

Heel

Shoe   Quarter   Toe

slightly differently, the farrier will trim and balance the foot to support the horse's movement. The shoes will be fitted by either hot or cold shoeing. For hot shoeing, each shoe is heated in a furnace and held for a short time against the hoof. This leaves an imprint that shows the farrier what adjustments to make so that each shoe makes the best possible fit to each hoof. Because the horse's hoof continually grows, the horse will need to be shod approximately every six weeks. For the same reason, the unshod horse also needs regular farriery attention to ensure that the shape and condition of the hoof is maintained.

Daily care

Daily hoofcare involves picking out the horse's feet with a hoof pick to remove dirt and stones, checking the condition of the shoe for wear, inspecting the sole for any evidence of punctures or bruising caused by stepping on sharp stones or a nail, and feeling for heat as a warning of infection or laminitis.

Abscesses can grow quickly inside the foot and cause immediate lameness. At the first sign of a puncture wound, no matter how small, the hoof needs to be dressed with a poultice and bandaged for at least 24 hours to draw out any infection.

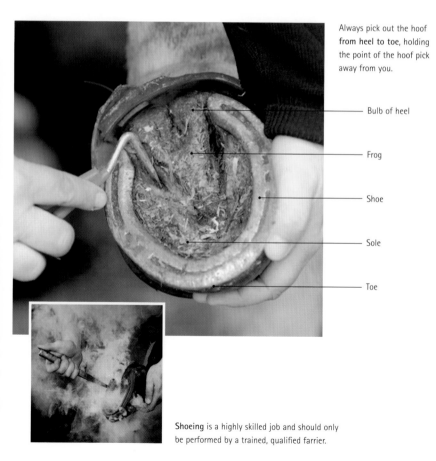

Always pick out the hoof from heel to toe, holding the point of the hoof pick away from you.

Bulb of heel

Frog

Shoe

Sole

Toe

Shoeing is a highly skilled job and should only be performed by a trained, qualified farrier.

WORMING

Regular removal of droppings from the pasture is an effective method of controlling worms.

It is impossible to eradicate worms in the horse's body altogether, so the main aim when worming is to control and reduce the number of worms.

Worm life cycle

Worm eggs can lie dormant in pasture for months until being eaten by the horse while grazing. The larvae then survive in the gut wall before hatching and living inside the body as parasites. Once they have matured, the worms lay eggs in the intestines, which

are then passed out of the horse's system in the dung. They remain in the pasture until being eaten by a horse, and the cycle starts again.

Reducing the worm burden

Effective worm control requires a program involving all horses living together, particularly where they are grazed together. It is a futile exercise to worm one animal and then turn it back out to pasture with other untreated horses as re-infection will take

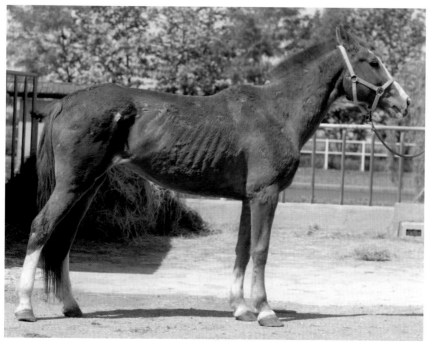

Left unhindered, worms will seriously compromise the horse's health, causing diarrhea, weight loss, respiratory problems and, in extreme cases, colic or irreversible damage to the intestines.

place immediately. All horses should be given the same worming product and care should be taken that the correct dose is given for each horse's weight, height and age. Over- or underdosing a horse encourages resistance in the worm population and lessens the impact of the drug, so administering the right quantity is important.

Good pasture management is also essential for controlling the worm burden. It is good practice to remove all droppings from the field on a regular basis to help break the worm life cycle. Grazing the pasture with cows or sheep can also be useful as they eat the eggs while grazing but are not suitable hosts for horse worms.

Signs of worm infestation

Classic signs of worm infestation in horses include a rough and dull coat, a "pot belly" where the horse's ribs can be seen clearly

while the stomach appears extremely tight and swollen, stunted growth and weight loss. Worms are not just restricted to the stomach of the horse but can live in many areas of the body, including the lungs, symptoms of which are coughing, nasal discharge and a raised temperature. Therefore, to be at their optimum peak health and performance, it is vital that all horses are regularly wormed.

> **HINT**
>
> Worming should be undertaken on a regular basis to be effective, usually every six weeks or three months depending on the worming product used.

TEETH

A horse's jaws and teeth are extraordinary. They begin to show when a foal is a few months old and grow constantly upward until the horse is 25 or 30 years old. They are perfectly designed to match its lifestyle as a feral pasture animal, as the action of grazing and chewing between 16 and 18 hours a day wears down the growing teeth. In addition, the grass eaten contains silica, which is naturally abrasive, so the wide variety of coarse grass and forage available in the wild keep the horse's teeth healthy, even into old age.

Domestication of the horse has not always been to its advantage—its grazing is restricted to relatively soft grass in limited areas; the horse is kept in a stable for long periods of time, often with nothing to eat for several hours; it is fed concentrated cereals and hayage, neither of which challenge its remarkable and inbred instinct to chew. Without the abrasive silica and rough forage to grind down the enamel, the horse's natural sideways chewing action encourages the teeth to spread out at the top. This results in uneven wear on the teeth and produces a razor-sharp edge on the outside of the tooth that can dig into the cheeks, causing painful ulcers and abscesses.

At 5 years the horse has permanent central, lateral and corner incisors.

At 7 years a hook is noticeable and cup marks (ring or inner teeth) begin to fade.

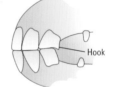

Hook

At 10 years the slope of teeth is increased and, in plain view, they are more triangular.

At 20 years a horse's teeth will be clearly sloping and grooves may be visible in the corner incisors.

Groove

Signs of dental problems
- Horse becomes head shy or dislikes wearing bits and nosebands.
- Problems arise during riding, such as head shaking, head tilting, opening the mouth or bucking, as the horse takes action to avoid the pain it is experiencing inside its mouth.
- Quidding—dropping half-chewed food from the mouth.
- Reluctance to eat, not finishing food or eating slowly.
- Loss of weight and condition.
- Undigested food in droppings.

Preventing dental problems
To prevent dental problems, the horse should have its teeth checked by a professional vet at least every six months. Any sharpness or uneven wear is filed back ("floated") to balance the mouth.

Telling age from the teeth
It is possible to accurately tell the age of a horse up until it is eight years old and to be able to estimate it for at least five years afterward.

Removing the sharp edges or hooks from a horse's teeth.

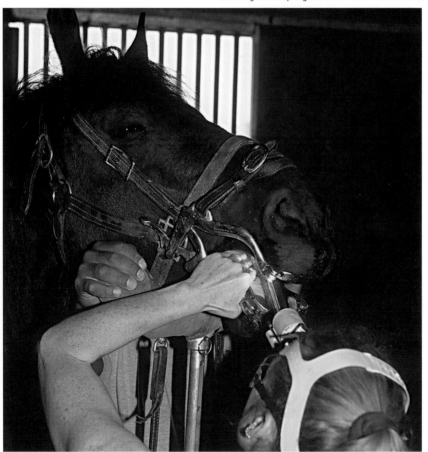

VACCINATIONS

Horses are vaccinated against a variety of diseases, including tetanus, equine influenza and rabies, depending on the country where you reside. Tetanus is usually fatal and is caused by bacteria spores in the soil and environment entering the horse's system via a wound. Equine influenza is a highly infectious virus that spreads rapidly from horse to horse in epidemic proportions. Rabies is a viral disease and is fatal by the time symptoms appear.

The process of vaccinating introduces a foreign substance into the horse's body that stimulates its immunity. The actual act of injecting the horse normally passes without incident, but occasionally it can cause a reaction in itself—horses can suffer from listlessness, mild discomfort, swelling

at the injection site or, in extreme cases, can become quite ill and depressed over a number of days. To avoid such side-effects the horse must not be worked hard or made to sweat for at least four days after the vaccination. Any stressful situations, such as traveling or moving to a new yard, should also be avoided at this time. Evidence of side-effects such as sweating or listlessness should be reported to the vet immediately.

Although no vaccine is 100 percent effective, if a disease is contracted, the reaction should be either prevented or reduced so that the horse recovers quickly. Horses that contract a disease should be kept isolated until they are fully recovered from the symptoms, even after vaccination, as they could still carry and pass on the infection.

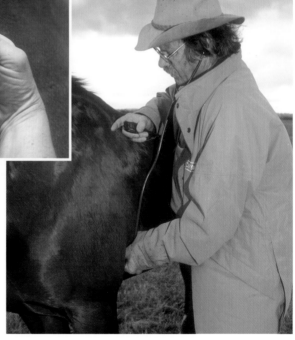

All equestrian societies require members to keep their horses up to date with vaccinations before attending any competitions or pleasure riding trials.

Each horse you own should have its own passport or certificate that contains details of its markings, age, name and date of birth. The passport also contains a record of the horse's vaccination history, which must be verified and signed off by a veterinary surgeon each time a horse is vaccinated.

Competitors are required to produce a passport to gain entry to equestrian events where evidence of current vaccinations is needed by the sport's ruling body. The passport must be kept with the horse all its life and should be passed on to a new owner if the animal is sold.

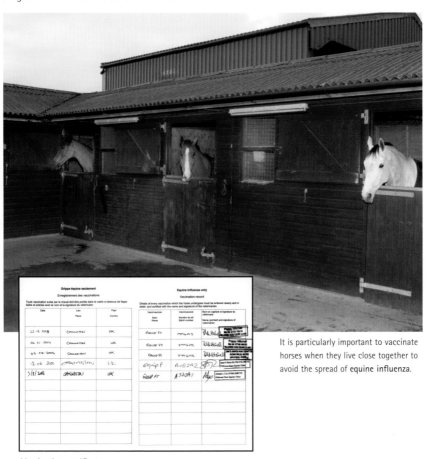

It is particularly important to vaccinate horses when they live close together to avoid the spread of **equine influenza**.

Vaccination certificate

HINT

Make sure that all vaccinations are kept up to date. If you fail to do this, your equine society will refuse to allow you to take part in its competitions and you will need to restart your vaccination program from the initial booster course.

PASTURE MANAGEMENT

A well-maintained field provides maximum grazing for horses.

Keeping horses at grass requires careful and thoughtful use of the available land. Horses are extremely fastidious spot grazers—they prefer to eat the most succulent shoots close to the ground and never eat near their own droppings. A classic example of pasture grazed by horses would show areas that are very overgrazed and patches with long grass that are virtually untouched. This wasteful use of grass leads some people to dismiss fields as just "turnout" places for horses rather than being useful sources of forage, or to think that there is plenty of grass available when in reality the horse does not have enough. Therefore good pasture management should aim to maximize the grazing potential of the land on which the horse lives.

The best way to improve your horse's grazing is to be proactive. Regularly cut or "top" the grass during the summer months to keep the length below 8 in (20 cm), which makes it more palatable for horses to eat. This has the added advantage of keeping weeds such as docks, buttercups and creeping thistles at bay. Ground-covering weeds such as these spread and reseed

rapidly, drawing nutrients out of the soil, smothering the grass and generally making the land very unproductive. It is good practice to spray a field once a year with a weed killer to keep on top of such invading weeds—spring is the optimum time when weeds are growing vigorously and the uptake of weed killer is greatest.

The other enemy of grassland is hoof traffic, particularly during winter months when overgrazing and wet conditions can lead to severe "poaching" (trampling or cutting up) of the pasture. Minimize this by decreasing turnout time or using temporary fencing to create a smaller "sacrifice area" on which to keep the horses while the rest of the field is allowed to recover.

Horses are very clean animals and will only leave droppings in certain parts of the field—such parts then become the roughest and least grazed areas. Regular collection of droppings will prevent these areas from becoming larger and disused and also provide an opportunity to regularly monitor the whole field, taking into account any litter or holes that may affect the horse's health or well-being.

Inedible, invasive
weeds can quickly
take over a field and
reduce the amount of
available grazing.

Because of their regular use, **gateways** are particularly
prone to poaching in winter.

Ragwort contains alkaloids that poison
the liver. There is no specific treatment
and the effects are usually fatal. It
should be methodically removed from
pastures by either spraying in spring or
being dug out manually.

105

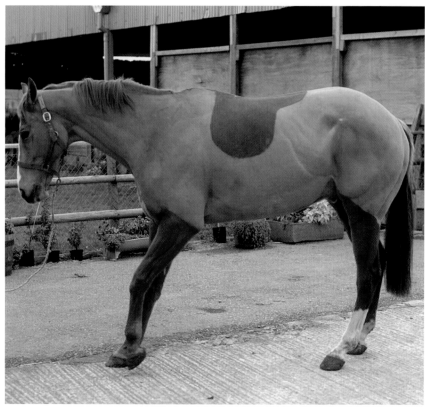

A typical stance for a horse with **laminitis**.

Laminitis

Laminitis is an extremely painful condition of the foot. Changes in the circulation cause inflammation of the sensitive laminae. Symptoms include leaning back by taking the weight on the heels in order to relieve pressure inside the hoof, a marked reluctance to move, heat in the hoof and increased pulse. Some horses and ponies are prone to suffering from laminitis so good management practices need to be put into place when caring for them. Lush, fast-growing grass and high quantities of hard feed are the biggest contributors. It is therefore important to monitor pasture during the spring and autumn and to remove the horse from grass altogether if necessary and feed hay.

Colic

Colic is severe abdominal pain and can occur for a variety of reasons. Symptoms include kicking at the belly, pawing the ground, sweating, lying down and rolling, fast and shallow breathing and groaning. Because of their long necks, horses are physically unable to vomit food that does not agree with them. Therefore, any feed must be appropriate for the animal and given in regular small portions rather than as one large feed that will overload the horse's gut. Avoid sudden changes in the diet. A regular worming program should be put in place to keep the horse's stomach and intestines as healthy as possible. Always allow food to settle for at least 1.5 hours before riding as the stomach

A horse suffering from **colic**.

is positioned very close to the lungs and will be directly affected by the increased expansion and contraction of the lungs.

Grass sickness

Grass sickness (equine dysautonomia) is a distressing and untreatable illness with no known cause that affects the horse's nervous system. It is most commonly seen in horses aged between three and seven years. Symptoms include muscle tremors, sweating, a high pulse rate and difficulty swallowing. The incidence is higher in spring and early summer, making those animals recently turned out after winter more at risk. The disease does not spread to cattle or sheep so the suggested cause may be a plant toxin that only creates a reaction in horses. Some regions hold more of an incidence than others. Questionable fields should not be grazed by horses and do not feed hay that has been cut from them.

This horse with **grass sickness** is showing weight loss and is clearly tucked-up.

107

CHOOSING THE RIGHT STABLE

Stables are not the natural environment for a horse but it is often necessary and more practical to keep your horse stabled. Bearing all the below points in mind, it is not necessarily the most expensive stable that offers a relaxed and healthy environment for the horse but the one that has had the most thought put into it.

Basic needs for a stable

A stable must meet the needs of your horse's safety and well-being:

- Sturdiness—it must be able to withstand all weather conditions.
- Size—10 ft by 10 ft (3 m by 3 m) for a pony; 14 ft by 12 ft (4 m by 3.5 m) for a large hunter. It should provide sufficient room for your horse to turn round or lie down without causing injury.
- Floor—should be safe, non-slip and level, and allow for being disinfected and swept.
- Door—must be sturdy and easy to operate. The horse should be able to see out over it at all times.
- Light—research shows that horses stabled in dark or dim areas develop more behavioral problems such as windsucking or box walking than those kept in plenty of natural light. Make sure your stable has a plexiglass window or plastic skylight.
- Drainage—ensure the proposed site is on well-drained ground.

Typical, **purpose-built** stables

Field shelter openings must be wide enough to allow access to all the horses that use it.

Location

Care must be taken over the proposed location for your stable. The ideal situation is to face away from the prevailing wind, preferably with the stable door facing the right way to catch the most of the morning sun (south to southeast in the northern hemisphere; north to northeast in the southern). Also make sure the stable is sited well away from hay or straw stacks as these can present a fire risk.

Amenities

Amenities are another factor to be considered. Your horse will need fresh running water plus electricity and lighting. Feed and bedding will need to be kept within reasonable distance of the stable, so bear in mind access for delivery vehicles.

Field shelters

The same basic needs for a stable apply to a field shelter. The shelter must have a minimum of three sides and be large enough to house all the horses in the field. Some horses can be quite territorial, so a large front opening is necessary to prevent one horse from standing guard and keeping the others outside.

Ventilation

Horses are extremely intolerant to the two Ds: drafts and dust. Stale air laden with dust spores from hay and straw can cause serious damage to the horse's lungs, so while effective ventilation is essential, it must be positioned high in the stable and designed to encourage a healthy circulation of fresh new air without its blowing around the horse's body.

BEDDING

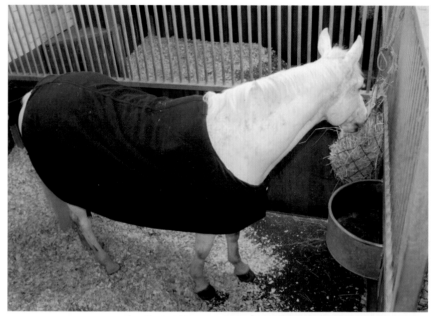

A stable should have **enough room** for the horse to move around and lie down easily.

A stabled horse requires a good supply of bedding to:

- Encourage it to lie down and rest.
- Reduce the likelihood of injury when lying down.
- Provide warmth and insulation from drafts.
- Reduce the jarring effect of standing on a hard surface for long hours.
- Help keep him and his rugs clean.

Bedding materials

- *Straw.* This is the most traditional bedding material. It makes a warm, comfortable, free-draining bed. Its advantages are that it is usually easily available, relatively cheap to buy and easy to dispose of. Disadvantages are that quality varies greatly and it can contain high levels of dust and fungal spores, it is not suitable for horses or owners who suffer from respiratory illnesses, and it is not suitable for horses who eat their bedding.

Straw makes a nice warm bed but can contain dust and fungal spores.

Rubber matting with shavings. Rubber is dust-free but works best when used with another material such as shavings.

Paper provides a dust-free bed but can cause staining.

- *Shavings.* This makes a clean, comfortable and absorbent bed that is easy to manage. It is often used for horses that suffer from respiratory diseases or that tend to eat straw beddings. The quality of the shavings can vary but dust-extracted shavings are available with low dust content. Its good absorbency properties make it a useful bedding for deep litter systems. It is usually available in polyethylene-wrapped bales, which makes storage easier.
- *Shredded wood fiber.* This is virtually dust-free, free-draining but absorbent. It moves around less than shavings. It is also available in polyethylene-wrapped bales for easy storage.
- *Rubber matting.* This is completely dust-free and provides good support for hooves and limbs. It is best used with another bedding material on top to help soak up urine and contain droppings. If used without another bedding, it can lead to wet floors, dirty rugs and horses, and requires a high standard of hygiene to avoid a build-up of ammonia.
- *Paper.* This makes a dust-free, absorbent bed. It is usually available shredded into long strips or diced into small pieces. Paper beds are usually less easy to manage than straw or shavings. They are usually made from printed paper and can cause staining. As it is lightweight, paper can easily be blown around the yard.

Bed management

It is essential that your stable is kept clean and hygienic at all times. There are three options:

- *Full muck-out.* Daily removal of all droppings and wet bedding.
- *Deep litter system.* Droppings are removed daily but not the wet bedding. The old bed is left undisturbed and covered with fresh bedding each day. A deep litter bed may stay down for as long as six months and will then need to be completely removed.
- *Semi-deep litter system.* Droppings are removed daily, leaving the removal of wet bedding to be done possibly once or twice a week.

With the exception of a deep litter bed, bedding should occasionally be moved to the sides of the stable and the floor left bare for a few hours to allow it to dry out.

GROOMING

In the wild, horses will naturally groom each other using their front teeth to scratch out any loose hairs along the body and to stimulate the skin underneath. As in many mammal social groups, grooming is necessary for health, warmth, status and as a means of bonding with other members of the herd. For the domestic horse the concept is the same.

Why groom?

Grooming is an excellent opportunity to spend time relaxing with your horse and developing a sense of trust and companionship. It is also an essential part of good horse management. Apart from making the horse look sharp, it keeps the animal healthy by removing accumulated dust, dead skin and hair, and helps maintain open and clean pores. Regular grooming of the whole horse also gives you the opportunity to familiarize yourself with the horse's body and to develop a keen eye for the sudden appearance of any abnormalities or abrasions. Although a stabled horse should be groomed daily before and after riding, a grass-kept horse does not need as much attention.

The grass-kept horse

During colder winter months it is important not to use a body brush on any horse that is living outdoors. The finishing action of the brush flattens the coat and removes both the vital insulating fluffiness and the natural waterproof grease from the coat.

HINT

An immaculately groomed horse is a real showstopper, a reflection of your horse-management skills and something in which to take enormous pride.

A **vigorous grooming** serves as a massage and can improve muscle tone.

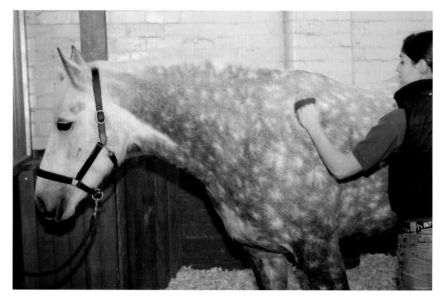

HOW TO GROOM

The grooming kit: (1) body brush, (2) dandy brush, (3) rubber curry comb, (4) scraper—used for removing mud and loose hair, (5) face brush, (6) hoof pick, (7) mane pulling comb, (8) mane and tail comb, (9) sweat scraper—used to remove sweat and water from the coat.

There are many tools on the market for grooming but the main four are a rubber curry comb, a stiff-bristled dandy brush, a soft-bristled body brush and a hoof pick.

Begin by using the rubber curry comb, rubbing it over the horse's body in circular motions with enough pressure to loosen dirt from the coat and bring it to the surface. As a rule, this is only done on the "soft" parts of the horse—the neck, sides and rump. Do not use the curry comb over the more bony areas of the legs and face as it will cause discomfort.

Next, use the dandy brush to work over the same area in the direction of the hair using a "flicking" motion to flick away the dirt from the horse and into the air. Finish the coat by grooming all over the horse with the body brush. This will lay the coat flat and give it a shine.

Complete your grooming by picking out the feet with a hoof pick, firmly moving from heel to toe without damaging the sensitive frog area (see *Hoofcare* on pages 96–97).

A **well-cleaned-out** hoof.

CHECKLIST FOR HEALTH

It is a good idea to familiarize yourself with the signs of a healthy horse as this makes it easier to identify signs of pain or infection in their early stages. To keep a horse healthy, it is vital to know how it looks, feels and behaves normally, so spend time watching and just being around your horse to help you understand and recognize its usual behavior.

Behavior
Horses are naturally very bright and alert. They are curious animals and show a great interest in their surroundings.

Ears and eyes
Ears should always have great mobility and prick quickly toward any new sights

Ears indicate a horse's interest in its environment and should always turn toward sights and sounds of interest.

or sounds. The eyes should be clear, bright and free of any discharge. The same applies to the nostrils, although a small amount of clear fluid is acceptable.

Coat and condition

The coat ought to be clean and have a good shine with healthy, supple skin underneath. During the warm summer months the coat will lie completely flat, but during the winter it will naturally stand out—a mechanism for trapping air between the hairs for extra warmth. A horse in good condition should have an adequate covering of fat over all its body but not to an excessive level. The best indicator of this is to be able to see just the outline of the ribs without being able to feel them easily.

Clear, bright eyes are a good sign of health.

Appetite

Most horses enjoy their food and display a good appetite. Droppings should be passed regularly, be brownish in color, and break easily upon hitting the ground.

Body processes

The breathing rate of a resting horse is barely noticeable at 8–16 breaths per minute. When at rest, the heart rate/pulse should be at its slowest, with a normal range of 32–48 beats per minute. The body temperature is taken via the rectum and should remain constant at between 98.6–100.4°F (37–38°C). Any increase in these statistics is an indicator of poor health and must be closely monitored.

Good management

It is good practice and more cost-effective to maintain your horse's health. A regular worming program, teeth care, vaccinations and hoof rasping are all necessary regardless of whether the horse is ridden or a retired companion.

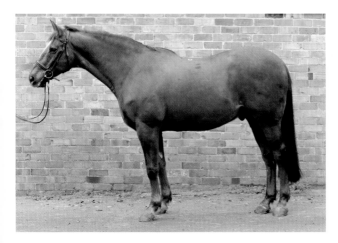

Careful observation and good management practices should lead to a healthy, happy horse.

WHEN TO CALL THE VET

An unusual stance such as this may indicate a health or injury problem.

As previously mentioned, it is always best if you are able to identify the signs of a healthy horse so they can act as a benchmark. If you spend time with your horse, you will quickly learn what is normal behavior for it and what is not. This knowledge will help tremendously when you need to decide whether or not to call in a vet. The important rule is: "If in doubt—do." Getting early veterinary advice can often save many complications and expenses later on.

Appetite

Any change in the horse's eating habits is an indication that something could be wrong. A good feeder that loses its appetite is a cause for concern.

Behavior

Any behavior that deviates from the horse's normal pattern should be noted.

- Horses are such sensitive animals that it is easy to see even from a long way off when something is wrong. A lame or injured horse in the field usually stands in an awkward stance—hunching its body and holding its head and neck low but without grazing.
- A group of horses generally act as a herd, so a horse standing away from the group or that is uninterested in the behavior of its companions is not usual.
- When being ridden, the onset of head tossing or bucking could indicate discomfort in the mouth or from saddlery.

Vet examining a horse

Discharges

Cloudy or thick discharge from the nostrils or eyes is a cause for concern, as is any respiratory noise or frequent coughing.

Problems with limbs

Any swelling or heat in the limbs can indicate a problem and may be the result of infection, strain or injury. Lameness can be detected by watching a horse being trotted away from and toward you—watch for the hindquarters to sink on one side or the head to nod as a foreleg touches the ground.

Body processes

Any increases in breathing rate, heart rate/ pulse or body temperature must be closely monitored.

Sweating

Patchy sweating on the horse's body (normally around the flanks), increased breathing rate and a dull coat that appears to stand on end are usually a sign of pain.

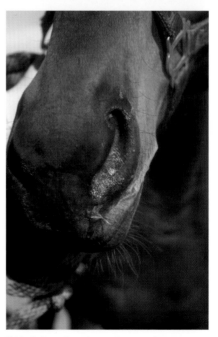

Thick discharge from the nose is a cause for concern.

A HOLISTIC APPROACH

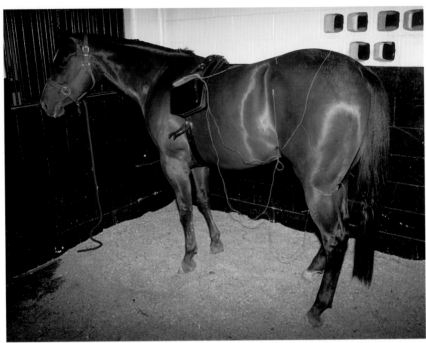

Acupuncture treatment is now more
commonly used on horses.

Holistic healthcare is often considered to be a modern-day phenomenon but, in fact, it has been used successfully on both humans and animals in the East for thousands of years. Our recent dependence on chemical medicines during the last century has contributed to making the re-emergence of alternative cures so extraordinary to us. Today, although still treated with suspicion by some vets, holistic practices are considered to be helpful in solving negative character traits and physical injuries in horses. Even if you are considering using holistic healthcare, professional veterinary advice should still be sought.

Horses respond well to holistic cures; indeed, a horse living in the wild will actively seek out certain plants and herbs with antiseptic properties or for pain relief. The domesticated horse, however, lives in a reduced acreage and relies solely on its owner for feed, nutrition and healthcare.

As equestrian feed companies become more sophisticated, they are developing many good herbal remedies for horses, such as nettle and celery seeds to soothe stiff joints, and raspberry leaf and St. John's wort to balance mares' hormones during the breeding season. All of these and more, such as arnica gel for lumps and bruises or tea tree oil as a natural antiseptic for cuts, are highly effective and popular among modern horse owners.

Magnotherapy is now well regarded in the equestrian world. It consists of a force field of magnets that trigger electrical impulses and directly affect the flow of blood around the body. Magnets are applied to targeted areas such as the lower leg to increase blood supply and speed up the recovery time. A further positive side-effect is the soporific effect of the magnets, which can help to calm and relax tense horses at competitions or when traveling.

Magnotherapy rug

The use of acupuncture in the Western world is now very widespread, especially in the United States, where racehorses are commonly treated to help them achieve optimum performance. The benefits of acupuncture can go far beyond simple pain relief and it is generally accepted as a cure for reproductive and hormonal problems in mares, chronic lameness, neurological problems and good for generally providing comfort and balance for the horse to give it a more relaxed outlook.

Solarium treatment is a common method for helping muscle healing and general toning and injury recovery.

THE RIGHT APPROACH

Be proud of yourself
Learning to ride is as much a mental feat as a physical one. Many people would not consider mounting a large animal, let alone moving freely around on one, so that very first step is an accomplishment in itself. Horses are strong-minded animals and it is impossible to ride them through domination alone, so progress at any level will need patience, self-awareness and a real understanding of how horses think and react to their environment.

Have goals
The key to developing the right approach to riding is a willingness to learn and, as your skills develop, the ability to take advice and utilize it. Confidence can easily be lost, so regular lessons with a qualified instructor are vital to ensure that you keep on the right track and make progress. You are more likely to improve if you have goals to work toward, such as being able to jump a small course of fences or mastering a new dressage movement such as leg yielding. Discuss

Riding can be enjoyed at all levels. **Hacking in the countryside** and enjoying the fresh air is a good goal to have.

When learning to ride, **the support of a group** of like-minded people is a valuable asset.

this with your instructor and work out an achievable timescale for meeting your target.

Group learning
Learning in a group can be very valuable, particularly if everyone is of a similar standard to you. A lot can be gained by watching others ride, and the conversational support from like-minded people will be an enormous benefit as you continue to progress.

Have an open and positive mind
Keeping an open and positive mind is essential when learning to ride. A lesson that all riders learn early in their riding careers is that what might have been easy to achieve on one horse, may be extremely difficult on another. Horses are great levelers and pay no

heed to their rider's age or status—they react according to the quality of the directions they are given. Horses do not deliberately aim to obstruct you, although it may feel like that at times! You are the leader in the partnership and you need to persevere until both of you get it right.

Don't put pressure on yourself
The beauty of riding is that you can have as much fun sitting quietly in the saddle walking along country lanes as you can practicing complicated dressage movements in an arena. Not all riders have to progress to jumping high fences or galloping around a cross-country course—it is just a question of deciding what level you are happy and confident with and learning to ride well enough to enjoy that.

ACQUIRING ADVANCED SKILLS

Having fewer lessons but taking them with a **top-class coach** may be worth considering.

As with any skill, improving your riding to a more advanced level will take a lot of time and practice but is achievable if you have the strength of mind to succeed. As a starting point, discuss your aims with your instructor, who will advise you how much work needs to be done and if the horse you currently ride is suitable for these plans.

The right horse

If you are serious about advancing your riding, then having a suitable horse will really help you move forward. Horses are very individual in their temperament and talents, and you will need a horse that has the right attitude and ability to meet the demands of your increased skills. It may be worth considering whether a horse with more experience and a higher level of training than you would help your development.

When learning something for the first time, it is much easier if your horse already knows what to do. Such horses are usually referred to as "schoolmasters" and are often over 10 years of age.

Taking lessons

Regular lessons are essential, and private tuition is preferable to group lessons. Do not be afraid to vary your instructor occasionally as a fresh pair of eyes can make a difference to your technique. You may find that it is worthwhile to have fewer lessons but to train with a top-class coach, who will give you a lot of exercises to practice in between your lessons. If you become stale with your riding, try something completely different—for example, a few show-jumping lessons can really improve the paces and transitions of a dressage horse and rider.

The right mental approach

So much of riding is psychological, and nerves or tension can play a large part in holding back some riders from their goals, especially during competitions. It is worthwhile taking the time to learn relaxation techniques and building them into your riding time. There are plenty of equestrian books and DVDs on the market alongside the more traditional approach to schooling and riding horses that can help you achieve this. All of them will give you valuable insight and the inspiration to keep progressing.

Watching the professionals

The beauty of riding is that you can excel with your horse in so many different environments, such as dressage, show-jumping, cross-country, endurance, mounted games or Le Trec. Attending any of these equestrian events as a spectator will give you an idea of the standard to aim toward. You will notice that top riders come in all shapes and sizes and display very different riding styles, all of which can be successful. Watching how they warm up their horses before competing will teach you a lot about technique and show you that there are no secrets to riding success—just tremendous amounts of patience, hard work and determination.

A rider competing in **a three-day event**.

ADVANCED RIDER FITNESS

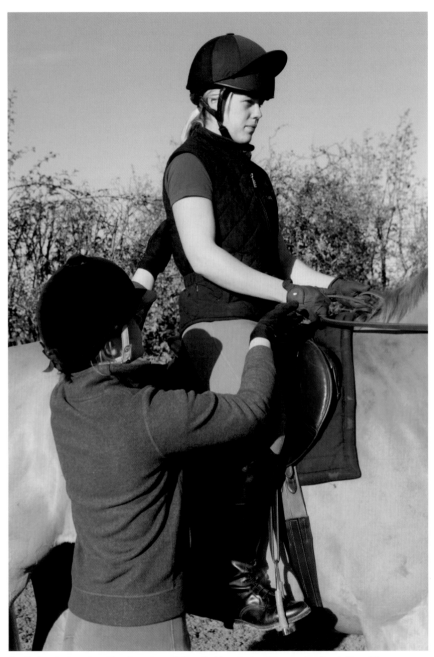

Developing stamina, strength and suppleness is important in order to achieve good posture in the saddle.

The most common misconception about riding is that "you just sit there," and watching top riders competing on television does nothing to dispel this myth. A professional rider who has spent many hours practicing with their horse will have developed all the essential muscles needed for riding, and will demonstrate such a close partnership with their mount that they appear to communicate through their minds rather than their bodies.

Many people are surprised at how physical riding actually is, especially during trot and canter work. The addition of nerves can leave riders feeling even more breathless, particularly when beginning to jump fences. Learning to ride is a gradual process and, if taken at the right pace, the body adapts positively to the demands being made of it. However, there are various exercises that can be carried out that will make the experience much easier.

Cardiovascular fitness

Increasing general aerobic fitness will improve your athleticism and prevent you from tiring so quickly. Exercises such as swimming, cycling and jogging are all useful in building up stamina. Start by introducing at least one of these workouts for half an hour once a week, gradually building up to three half-hour sessions a week over time. This will greatly help to improve your fitness and make you feel much more comfortable during and after riding.

Suppleness and lower-back strength

Lower-back strength is vital. Much of the subtle control seen in advanced riders takes place in this area, so increasing core body strength is of great benefit. Classes in Pilates and yoga are excellent preparation for riding as they stretch muscles and build strength throughout the whole body without adding bulk. In addition, they encourage suppleness in the hip, knee and ankle joints, which aids stability on the horse and improves the shock absorption necessary for jumping. Because supple joints and good upper-body posture are so important, many riders study the Alexander technique. This helps them to sit correctly and dispels postural bad habits that can haunt some established riders for years.

Mental strength

Another important factor in rider fitness is the mental strength required to cope with riding large horses often in stressful situations, such as at competitions or in busy traffic. Horses are enormously sensitive creatures and respond to every tiny movement and emotional reaction produced by their rider. This can work against us when we are nervous but it is also why eventually we are able to ride without seeming to move. Learning relaxation skills and generally building up confidence around different horses will go a long way toward establishing your mental fitness and will continue to make riding a real pleasure.

Pilates is excellent for strengthing the muscles that support the spine.

LUNGING

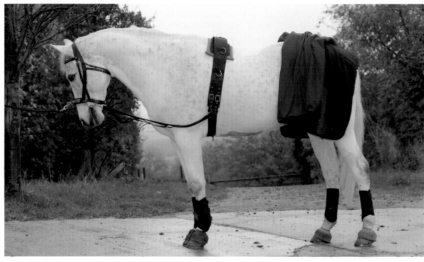

A horse in **full lunge equipment**.

When used correctly, lunging will improve the horse's fitness, flexibility, strength and obedience. It is an excellent all-round exercise and a good opportunity for you to watch your horse working from the ground. Lunging requires a quiet area with a safe, nonslip surface where you can work the horse on a circle up to 65 ft (20 m) in size.

Equipment
- Strong nylon lunge line at least 25 ft (7 m) long.
- Good-quality cavesson and/or snaffle bridle.
- Saddle or surcingle.
- Side reins.
- Lunge whip with long handle and lash.
- Protective boots for the horse.
- Riding hat and light, fitted gloves for you.

How to hold the lunge line
To lunge on the left rein, hold the lunge line in your left hand with the slack coiled loosely and the lunge whip in your right hand. At all times the whip must be kept a sensible distance from the horse and carried low to the ground. Some people prefer to hold the slack of the lunge rein in the same hand as the whip. Either way, you should be able to shorten or lengthen the line according to the size of the circle.

Your position
Your aim is for the horse to move on a circle around you. It is important to remain on the same spot in the center of the circle so that the horse walks a true circle. Turn your body in the same direction that the horse is moving. The horse is influenced by your position in relation to its body. You should aim to be the anchor of a triangle formed by the lunge line, the horse and the whip—your body should be opposite the saddle, the whip pointing at the hindquarters, and your horse's shoulders a little ahead of your body.

Voice commands
Lunging your horse is an effective method of establishing voice commands, and you should eventually be able to use your voice to control the horse on the lunge. The horse will respond to the tone of the voice rather than to actual words, so make all your commands clear, consistent and short. Use a rising tone for upward transitions (speeding up) and a long, drawn-out, descending tone for downward transitions (slowing down).

WARMING UP

It is important to keep you and your horse as calm as possible when lunging—if you feel nervous, ask an assistant to walk at the side of the horse's head for extra control until you are more confident.

- Use your voice command to ask the horse to move forward by saying "walk on" boldly. This can be supported by making an encouraging clicking noise with your tongue. The horse should move quietly away from you to the left, and you can release loops of the lunge line as he does so, making sure that they do not drag along the ground. If he does not walk on from your voice command, keep the whip low to the ground, pointing to his hindquarters, and shake it quietly, again saying "walk on." At this initial warming-up stage, it is important that the horse walks actively forward in

a relaxed manner in order to help him loosen his muscles. A good gauge of this is if the head remains reasonably low with ears pricked and the tail swings with each stride.

- Most of the warmup should be walked but some horses benefit from a little work in trot. To trot, firmly say, "ter-rot." To return to walk, give a calm, low voice command, "wa-alk."
- This stage of the warmup should last at least five minutes before asking for a halt. Do this by asking in a calm, low voice for the horse to "whoa" and also tucking the lunge whip under your right arm behind you as you do so.
- Once the horse has halted, turn him around to face the other direction and repeat the process, taking care not to tangle the lunge line. Complete a further five minutes of the warm-up in this direction.

LUNGING

Monitor your lunging style to improve your technique and provide clear communication with your horse.

This horse is starting to stretch forward and down.

Once the warmup has been achieved properly, there are many drills and exercises that can be carried out on the lunge.

Downward stretching
It is important to encourage a downward stretch in the horse's neck and back as, like any athlete getting their body ready for use, this will safely prepare the horse for more work later on. Keep a light but firm contact down the lunge line to the horse's head (use the lunge line in a similar style to your normal riding reins), and then release the contact slightly without giving it away all together. This will encourage the horse to drop its head forward and down toward the ground.

Horse being worked at walk.

As this happens, play the contact again by bringing your elbow gently back toward your side and wriggling your hand slightly from the wrist as if landing a fish. This exercise will encourage the horse to stay in this lower position. It will be necessary to repeat the exercise again at the end of the lunging session as you stretch and cool the horse down.

Flexion exercise
A simple exercise for improving the horse's flexion (flexibility) is to gradually increase and decrease the size of the circle the horse is working on. Do this by encouraging the horse to go forward in an active manner while shortening the lunge line by at least a foot to bring the horse onto a slightly smaller circle. Providing your body stays in the same place, this small change will adjust the horse's way of going.

After approximately one circle, release the lunge line again by the same amount to put the horse back onto the bigger circle. For maximum benefit, repeat the exercise in both directions at intervals in both walk and trot.

Improving the hindquarters
An exercise to improve the muscles in the hindquarters is to increase and decrease the pace as the horse works on the circle by encouraging a more forward and active gait for approximately half a circle before bringing it back to its original pace. This exercise can be carried out in both walk and trot.

Your lunging style
Carefully monitor your style when working horses on the lunge:
- Keep your movements to a minimum.
- Stay organized with the lunge line and whip.
- Practice shortening and lengthening the lunge line quickly so that the loops do not become tangled around your hands and feet.
- Use the lunge whip as discreetly as possible to avoid alarming the horse.

> **HINT**
>
> The horse can be worked on the lunge at walk, trot and canter, providing the ground conditions are safe.

LONG REINING

Long reining is commonly used to introduce young or unbroken horses to ridden work by allowing them to experience a bridle, bit and saddle without a rider. However, as any exercise that can be carried out in the saddle can also be achieved with long reining, it is a very useful way of training horses throughout their working life.

As with lunging, both you and horse can benefit—you can watch the horse performing the movements, while the horse gains a better understanding of the exercises before carrying a rider. Furthermore, the young horse is given the opportunity to gain strength and flexibility throughout its body prior to being ridden.

A rider warming up a horse—demonstrated here without saddle or surcingle.

Equipment
There are different types of long reining but here we shall focus on the English method, which involves using two reins of at least 30 ft (9 m) each. The horse should wear a saddle with the stirrup irons down at full length and secured together safely by a strap passing under the belly. This means that the leathers have been safely adapted for the reins to slip through. Alternatively, a surcingle can be worn that is secured firmly around the horse's girth region and has rings on either side for the reins to pass through.

The reins must be of equal length. They attach to the bit rings on either side of the bridle, then pass through the stirrups or the rings of the surcingle. The reins should be held in the same manner as when riding a horse. For safety, you should keep at a distance of at least 10 ft (3 m) from the horse at all times and wear gloves, sturdy boots and a hard hat.

Starting work

Encourage the horse to move forward on a large circle by using either your voice and the reins, or the whip. Keep the horse moving in a positive and active manner at all times. For everyone's safety, it is important to stay slightly to one side of the horse, where you will remain in its view, rather than standing directly behind—young horses in particular prefer to keep their handler in their sights.

Use experienced help

Always have an experienced professional with you when you first begin long reining as there is a lot to think about and large animals can be unpredictable, particularly when frightened or unsure of what is being asked of them. It is good practice to have an assistant walk at the horse's head to calm and direct it until it understands what you are asking it to do.

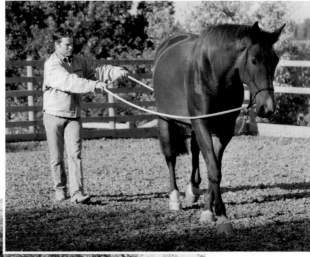

The rider always remains a safe distance away while remaining in the horse's view. For safety reasons, you should wear a helmet (hard hat) when long reigning.

Working actively forward in trot on a circle.

HINT

Before starting to long rein, spend time touching and rubbing the reins over the horse's body and moving around with them to get the horse used to the feel of the reins on its body.

LONG REINING

Circles

The initial aim of long reining is for the horse to move in a relaxed and forward-going manner. This is best achieved by working the horse in walk on a large circle at least 50 ft (15 m) in diameter. Big circles are ideal for training horses, particularly young ones, as they are large enough for the horse to keep its balance yet still encourage flexion from the side of its body on the outside of the circle by bending its body slightly to the inside. You must also keep walking in order to keep up with the horse and will need to use your voice, reins, position and, if necessary, the whip to control the horse's pace.

At this point, you are teaching the horse the basics of control and obedience. Working on a circle you should ask the horse to walk, trot and halt in response to your aids, aiming to make your aids gradually more discreet as the horse begins to understand what you are asking. It is rewarding to see how quickly a human and horse can build a trusting relationship between each other as these drills and exercises develop.

Serpentines and figure-eights

Once you and the horse are proficient with the aids, more complex movements such as a serpentine can be performed. The serpentine requires the horse to carry out a series of changes in direction while continually moving forward. Keep the horse in front of you at all times so that it can be steered to the left for half a circle then directed to the right and so on. Once you are competent with the serpentine, try performing figure-eights, but once again concentrating on control and encouraging a rhythmic, active pace from the horse at all times.

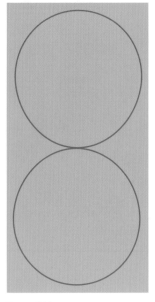

Figure-eight

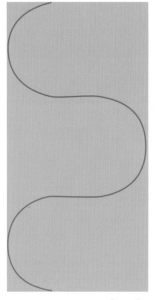

Serpentine

Encourage the horse to move **in a straight line** by walking along a fence.

Straight lines

Long reining work should also be done in straight lines. This is much harder than it appears as horses are very prone to "wobble" if they have not been taught to move straight without relying on assistance. Begin by walking the horse in a straight line alongside a wall or fence to keep him on a true line. Next, walk him approximately 1 foot (30 cm) away from the fence while still aiming to achieve a straight line.

Continue until the horse learns to move in a straight line without anything near him that he can use as a guide.

Standing still

One of the most important skills you can teach a horse is to stand patiently and still between exercises. This is vital for safety and also the foundation of good manners that will be a benefit to the horse for the rest of its life.

Standing still on long rein promotes obedience and good manners.

IMPROVING TRANSITIONS

A good-quality transition occurs when the horse changes its pace either upward or downward in a precise and calm manner. This is achieved through the rider's technique and depends on their ability to prepare the horse's mindset and way of going before asking for the change. If asked to make a transition without warning, the horse will naturally be surprised and either overreact by jumping forward too quickly, or not react at all. Therefore, the key to achieving a calm transition is the preparation.

Preparing the pace

A transition is only as good as the quality of the horse's pace or way of going before it. Therefore, when preparing to ride a transition, you must ensure that the current pace is forward, active and soft. To achieve this, you must have a light contact on the reins from the hands to the horse's mouth.

Holding this contact with your hands while playing with the bit slightly by squeezing with the fingers will invite the horse to soften its mouth and lower its head. Pressing your lower legs lightly and regularly against the horse's sides will ask it to move its body forward and in a rounded and active manner. Done together, these two actions encourage the horse to work forward and into the contact as well as it possibly can.

Forewarning the horse

As transitions are all about preparation, it is necessary to warn the horse that a transition is coming up by balancing and steadying it correctly. This is achieved by riding half-halts. There are several ways to ride the half-halt but a useful one is to sit up very straight in the saddle and then attempt, literally, to suck the horse up inside your body, starting from your knees and working upward toward

A well-balanced upward **transition to canter.**

Use your lower leg in a downward transition to ask the horse to move actively into the lower pace.

your chest. Hold this position for no more than five seconds. Each time you do this, the horse should check itself and readjust its pace. What you are doing is warning the horse that something is about to happen and it is responding by balancing its body and becoming slightly more collected in order to react promptly to your next command.

Making the transition
With the horse going forward and listening to you in this manner, it is easier for it to perform a transition. To ask the horse for an upward transition to the next pace, simply yield a little with your hands and squeeze firmly with your lower legs; to ask for a downward transition, hold the reins firmly with your hands and squeeze with the lower

legs so that the horse knows to drop actively to a lower pace.

Different types of transitions
- Progressive transitions—from walk to trot or trot to canter.
- Direct transitions—from walk to canter.
- Transitions within a pace—from a working trot to a collected trot, or lengthened strides during a medium walk.

HINT

Remember, preparation is key: Your horse needs to know in advance what you want it to do.

135

YOUR JUMPING SEAT

Rider in jumping position—lower leg taking the rider's weight, upper body folded forward.

The jumping position is used for three reasons:
- To stay up off the horse's back and avoid hindering it as it makes the "bascule" shape over a jump.
- To give the rider security and the ability to sit to any changes in balance that the horse might make during the movement.
- To allow the hands to move further up the horse's neck to avoid hurting its mouth as it lifts off.

To adopt this position, you will need to use your body like a pendulum—all your weight should be based in the lower part of the legs, while the top half of your body remains extremely lightweight and flexible. Your legs need to be reasonably strong to achieve this, so work toward building them up either through cycling or hacking with shorter stirrups, which will help to develop the calf and thigh muscles. This additional fitness will vastly improve your jumping seat, as it will give you the strength to balance evenly over the horse's back, particularly during cross-country events when the rider needs to assume the jumping position for much longer periods of time.

Your lower leg (from the knee down) is the anchor that will prevent you from becoming unseated. Take time to watch professional riders jumping on television or at competitions and notice how this part of

Staying off the horse's back as it jumps allows it to make the "bascule" shape necessary for good jumping.

the leg completely absorbs the movement yet never moves from the horse's side—aim to emulate this by holding your calf firmly against the saddle but without overgripping. To improve your stability further, as you adopt the jumping position, imagine heavy weights hanging from your lower body, pulling your waist and bottom backward toward the hind feet of the horse—this will encourage a deeper seat and keep your balance in direct proportion to the movement of the horse.

The jumping position is only assumed briefly while the horse is in the air over the fence: the rest of the time you should sit lightly in the saddle, maintaining a flexible upper body with relaxed shoulders, arms and wrists and keeping your hands low and still on the horse's neck.

An experienced rider tackling a cross-country course can make riding look like a real art form—their legs and bodies completely absorb the movements, and to an onlooker the rider hardly seems to move in the saddle. To ride like this is certainly something to aspire to.

HINT

Of course your weight can't change but "think light" as you rise from the saddle and cross the jump.

RIDING CLUB ACTIVITIES

Riding clubs are an excellent way of bringing together like-minded riders and horse-lovers from a local area. Originally, clubs were formed to provide a greater voice for equestrianism within a region and led campaigns to open up more trails and to improve riding and road safety. However, in recent years, as amateur equestrian activities have increased in popularity, riding clubs have really come into their own to make riding more accessible and provide a safe and educational environment for riders to enjoy their horses and meet new people. The emphasis at all times is on learning, fun and improvement.

A riding club show is an excellent way to meet other enthusiasts; it also gives both rider and horse an opportunity to take part in various activities.

Membership structure

Riding club activities cater to all types of people—from non-horse-owners or complete novices up to advanced riders. Junior membership typically applies from 10 to 17 years of age with senior membership from 18 years onward. Associate membership is available for people who do not own a horse, but there are always plenty of opportunities for non-horse-owners to be involved either through helping out at competitions, planning an event, or attending lectures and social functions.

All members must pay an annual fee. They must also complete a form, giving accurate details about themselves and their horses and information about their favorite equestrian pursuits so that the club can continue to provide the most popular kinds of activities.

Belonging to a club will open up opportunities—such as lectures on horsemanship—which are beneficial, informative and fun.

Membership benefits

Benefits of membership can include reduced entry fees to competitions, access to visiting trainers, subsidized training clinics and discounts from appropriate local businesses. All riding clubs pride themselves on running a professional and well-structured organization and will often affiliate themselves with much bigger national equestrian societies. This can bring additional benefits to members in the form of insurance cover and access to legal advice.

The newsletter

A well-organized club will provide a regular newsletter listing all its planned activities. These can include talks about riding and horse husbandry, visits to equestrian events, instructional riding clinics for each level of riding, and social events for members to get to know each other. Details of forthcoming competitions in dressage, show-jumping, trail riding or showing will often be included along with photos and results from previous events. Essentially, the riding club newsletter will be a voice for the local equestrian community with news reports and a classified section listing, among other things, horses for sale or wanted and trailers or horse trucks available to buy. Many larger riding clubs will have a website with active discussion forums to enable members to network with each other online.

HINT

By affiliating yourself with a club you can find out about a variety of upcoming equestrian events.

GYMKHANAS AND SHOWS

You must pay to enter your classes at the secretary's tent, which in this case has been set up in a horsebox. You must also wear your number clearly displayed in all your classes. This helps the judge to identify you.

If you have progressed in your riding and feel confident at trot, canter and jumping, then the next step is to enter some classes at a local show, where independent judges award rosettes and prizes to the winners. Horse shows and gymkhanas are held regularly during the summer, traditionally Sundays. You can find them advertised in local papers, in leaflets at your local tack shop or feed store and through riding clubs.

A horse show is a perfect opportunity to test your riding ability against other riders. All types of horses are welcome and there are classes to suit everyone. Competitors are required to wear the correct clothing, including cream jodhpurs, black riding boots, riding jacket and a riding hat that meets the current safety standards. It is also expected that you make a good effort to turn out your horse as well as you can, including plaiting its mane and tail if appropriate for your class. If the show is within hacking distance, then it may be convenient for you to ride there; otherwise, competitors normally transport their horses to events in horseboxes or trailers. On arrival, park alongside the other horseboxes, leaving plenty of space around the vehicle so that you can unload and prepare your horse for the event.

Gymkhana games are great fun for both ponies and riders.

Before the day of the show, study the schedule carefully and decide which classes you would like to enter. Some classes are straightforward showing where the horse and rider are judged on their style and presentation; other classes are purely show-jumping, starting with small novice classes at the start of the day and then increasing the height of the jumps for each class up to advanced level. There may be more than one show ring for the day, so make sure that your choices do not overrun each other and you do not have to rush from one class to the next. You will need to pay to enter your classes before they begin, so find the secretary's tent right away and they will write down which classes you have entered. The secretary will give you a number to wear that you should tie neatly around your waist or around the top of your arm. You should make sure to wear this number at all times in the show ring.

Gymkhanas are normally run in conjunction with a much bigger show and are an ideal opportunity for young children to enjoy their ponies at a show without having too much pressure put on their abilities. Popular classes include:

- The bending race, in which ponies bend between a series of poles.
- "Chase Me Charlie," where ponies jump over a fence that is raised higher each time.
- Handy pony class, where pony and rider complete a series of obstacles such as opening and closing a gate and placing bean bags inside a small bucket on the floor.

COMPETITION PREPARATION

If you are a keen rider, you will begin your preparation for a competition weeks or even months before the event. Depending on the type of competition you are entering, your horse will need regular training to become more flexible and obedient for dressage, more confident over fences for jumping, or much fitter and versatile to handle for endurance riding or Le Trec.

You will need to obtain a copy of the competition schedule from the show secretary. This will contain all the details of date, venue, classes and what rules the event will be run under. For some shows, you will need to send your entry and fees to the show secretary by a specified closing date. If you are entering a dressage competition, make sure you have a copy of the test you will be riding so that you can practice riding the movements and memorizing the test before the day.

In the two weeks prior to the event, check your horse's feet and book a farrier appointment in plenty of time if required. Begin gradually smartening up your horse by pulling its mane and tail or by increasing your grooming regime to ensure the coat will look its best on the day. Trim excess hair from around the horse's ears, muzzle and fetlocks with scissors or clippers.

A few days before the journey check your trailer or horsebox to avoid any unpleasant surprises such as a flat tire on the morning of the show. If appropriate, give your horse a good bath, including washing its mane and tail. This will give the healthy and shiny oils in its coat time to re-emerge.

On the day before the event, fill up your vehicle with gas, groom the horse thoroughly all over, and write a list of all the equipment you will need to take for both you and your horse—do not be surprised if it is long! As well as tack, rugs and a grooming kit, your horse will also need enough hay or feed and water to last for the whole time you are away from home. Decide if you are going to plait up the night before or first thing the next morning. Allow plenty of time to do this as it can take up to two hours to plait

Painting hooves is best done before departure. Take a touch-up kit with you for emergencies.

a horse for the first time. The dress code for horse events varies, so check the schedule, but you will need to be properly turned out, including a hair net and gloves, polished boots, cream jodhpurs and some spare clothes to change into should the weather turn wet.

Finally, do not forget the directions to the showground, money, cell phone, a packed lunch and, most importantly of all, plenty of time in which to get there!

HINT

The weather is an important consideration for horse and rider. Check ahead for such factors as possible rain, intense heat or cold nights.

There will be a lot to do on the day, so make sure you **arrive at your competition in plenty of time.**

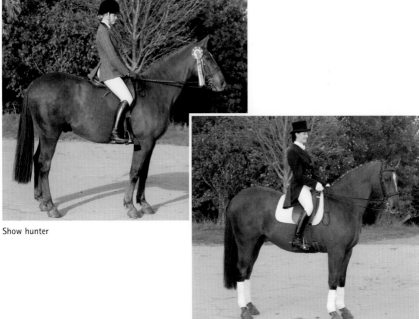

Show hunter

Dressage rider

PLAITING OR BRAIDING

Plaiting or braiding a mane and tail makes a horse look smart when appearing in a competition. It helps to show off their looks and conformation to the very best advantage. In some showing classes, certain breeds, such as purebred Arabs and mountain and moorland ponies, do not require plaiting—all of these are encouraged to have long, flowing manes and tails that accentuate their movement. However, for those horses that suit braiding, the results can be breathtaking.

PLAITING THE MANE

- Make sure to begin with a clean, well-pulled mane that has been combed over onto the horse's right-hand side and that is approximately 4–5 in (10–13 cm) long.
- Dampen the mane slightly with water and divide it into an odd number of equal sections from the withers to the poll, with the final plait in the forelock making an even number of plaits on the horse.
- Stand on a sturdy box and divide one section of mane into three smaller, equal strands.
- Begin to braid that section by tightly passing the right strand over the central one, then the left strand over the central one, and so on until the plait has been completed neatly.
- Fasten the end of the plait with either a small elastic band or needle and thread that matches the color of the horse's mane.
- Finish by rolling or doubling the plait up underneath itself until it is secured firmly at the base of the mane.

Section of mane ready to be plaited.

Tightly passing side strand over central strand.

Fasten the end of the plait with an elastic band.

Loose end fastened securely and a finished plait.

Enhancing the appearance

A horse's appearance can be much improved by clever plaiting:

- Create an optical illusion of features looking bigger and stronger by securing the plaits high up on the horse's neck.
- Plait close into the horse's neck to draw the attention away from too much bulk.
- Use several smaller plaits to make a neck look longer.
- Use fewer and bulkier plaits to add length to a short neck.

Practice makes perfect

A neatly plaited horse is a real sign of professionalism and it is well worth putting in the hours of practice at home to get the effect just right on the day. It can take up to two hours for a complete beginner to plait a horse, but an experienced groomer can prepare a horse's mane and tail in just over half an hour.

Tails

Although it is the current fashion for the tail to be neatly pulled, it is a great finishing touch to use a French plait from the base of the tail down the length of the dock, completed by fixing the remaining hair in a neatly plaited loop.

The end of the plait is tucked under and sewn into place with needle and thread to give a smart appearance.

A well-presented lineup.

The final results for **competition day**.

EVENTING AND HUNTER TRIALS

Because of the level of skill needed for three-day eventing, usually only professional riders take part.

The history of eventing

The popular sport of eventing has its roots in the education of military horses in the army and was originally designed as a test to train the ultimate cavalry horse. The calmness and precision necessary for a dressage phase was intended to emulate the horse on the parade ground, while the steeplechase and demands of the cross-country course mirrored the courage required by a charger on the battlefield. The final phase of show-jumping proved that, after such a feat of endurance, the horse was still able to demonstrate its health, soundness and agility by completing a series of up to 20 show-jumping fences without showing any ill-effects.

The three-day event

Eventing is popular all over the world but nowhere more so than in Great Britain, where the world-famous Badminton Three-Day Event is considered to be one of the most demanding courses ever constructed. The first day, normally a Friday, is dedicated to dressage, while the popular steeplechase and cross-country phase is always held on a Saturday. Spectators can walk around the course and watch horses and riders up close as they compete. Sunday, the final day, consists of a thorough veterinary inspection in the morning. For this, the event horses are turned out immaculately. Plaited up and with hooves oiled, they are presented for inspection, where they are led by their riders at walk and trot past a veterinarian, who judges the horses for condition and soundness. This section is very important—if any horse is not considered to be fit enough, it will not be able to compete in the final stage of the event, the show-jumping.

Throughout the competition, penalties are awarded for inaccuracies in the dressage, for refusals or time faults in the cross-country (from going too fast or too slow) and for fences knocked down or refused in the show-jumping. The overall winner is the horse and rider with the fewest penalties after the show-jumping phase. Because three-day eventing is so demanding, it is normally only attempted by professional riders. Smaller one-day events, where all the disciplines are completed at a much smaller scale during one day, are much more popular among amateur riders.

Hunter trials

Hunter trials are much more low-key and enjoyable events for the pleasure horse owner. Also known as steeple-chase, they consist of a series of fences that are jumped in a prearranged order in the open countryside. Horses and ponies of all abilities can enter—classes are available at different height levels, starting from novices with fences at 1 ft,

Inspection by a veterinarian will determine if a horse is fit enough for the final stage.

9 in (52 cm), up to advanced riders jumping 3 ft, 9 in (112 cm). The course covers an enormous variety of fences, including water jumps, brush fences and log piles. Riders are encouraged to arrive early and will initially walk the course on foot so they can familiarize themselves with the layout and approach to each fence.

Hunter trials are enormous fun and very popular with children as well as adults. Competitors wear brightly colored sweatshirts and matching silks on their hats and often combine their own chosen colors with that of their pony's numnah and protective boots. Safety back protectors are essential, as are gloves and a medical armband, which is worn by every competitor in case of an accident.

Pairs classes in hunter trials are enormous fun for horses and riders.

RIDING CLASSES

When taking part in pleasure riding classes, make any changes of pace on your own time rather than waiting for the other horses to begin—you need your horse to stand out as an individual.

Pleasure riding classes

The pleasure riding class is the most popular Western riding competition. Competitors are judged in a group rather than individually, and the emphasis is mainly on the horse, making pleasure riding an inviting and easy introduction to showing in the Western style. The key to the competition is in the title—the horse must look a pleasure to ride. The judges are therefore looking for a relaxed and easily controlled horse that is not worried by the environment of the show ring and the other horses around it.

A class begins with the competitors walking in a large circle around the judge. When appropriate, they are all asked via a loudspeaker to move forward at "jog" (trot). Next, the competitors will be asked to move upwards to "lope" (a very controlled canter).

At some stage, the riders will be asked to make their horses "reverse," which requires the horse to move backward in a straight line. The winner will be the most happy, relaxed horse with a good movement that appears to respond to almost invisible aids from the rider and can be ridden on a very loose rein.

Showmanship classes

In a showmanship class, the horse is used almost as a prop while the handlers take their turn to show how well they can control their horse from the ground. A predetermined set of moves is carried out in front of a judging panel. The moves are often only made known to the handlers an hour before the class begins. As the emphasis is on the handler, competitors wear very elaborate

Elaborately dressed competitors are part of the presentation necessary for showmanship classes.

Western-style costumes with starched jeans, boots, a belt with buckle, large cowboy hat and a highly decorated blazer—female competitors are even encouraged to wear plenty of makeup. Showmanship is really a fun class with the handler being judged on his or her ability to present the horse in the best possible manner to the judge. This means providing an unobstructed view of the horse throughout the routine yet always being in full control and demonstrating that the horse shows complete respect and will obey the slightest command.

Reining

Reining is a very impressive spectator sport and has its roots firmly in the history of American stock raisers. A good cattle-hand needs a highly responsive horse from which to round up and rope in ranch steers, one that can accelerate up to a gallop at the slightest encouragement, turn on a dime and stop absolutely still without a moment's hesitation—essentially a horse that is obedient and in tune with its rider. During a competition, riders are asked to perform a set pattern of movements in front of a panel of judges. Movements such as the famous "sliding stop," where the horse halts from gallop by locking its back legs firmly in place while running forward with its front legs until it stops, are inspiring to watch, while the "rollback turn," where the horse slides to a halt before immediately turning 180 degrees and setting off at a fast gallop again, makes for very dramatic viewing. Horses are judged on their speed, finesse and smoothness—and ultimately their relationship with the rider.

North American quarter horses are the best breed to use for a reining competition.

DRESSAGE

Dressage is a French word that means "training." It is a progressive way of teaching horses to move effortlessly under what appears to be minimal instruction from the rider. In fact, it is communication between horse and rider at its highest level. Horses are willing, natural athletes and will learn quickly from a professionally skilled dressage rider. Although some movements look extremely difficult for the horse to perform, it is important to realize that all dressage movements are based on the movements that a horse makes in its natural environment.

Dressage is an incredibly elegant sport both to watch and to participate in. The whole concept is to work horses without fear or force and without gadgets or equipment that may otherwise artificially enhance their movements. Tack is basic and unobtrusive, such as a snaffle bridle and a dressage saddle

that is cut to provide more length for the rider's leg and lies closer to the horse than ordinary saddles.

In competitions, horse and rider are always turned out immaculately. The horse should have a plaited mane, spotless tack and a saddle set off by a white numnah. Riders wear gloves, black polished riding boots and cream jodhpurs with either a black or tweed jacket topped off by a velvet hat that is cut in a flattering style for the wearer. At advanced and Olympic level, riders wear a black top hat, a jacket with tails and white jodhpurs. Being well turned out on show day displays respect and good manners toward the judge.

A dressage competition requires the horse and rider to complete a standard dressage test. The test consists of a series of set riding movements that have been prerehearsed in

A perfectly turned-out horse and rider create an elegant impression.

Judges award marks out of 10 for each movement of a dressage test and provide helpful comments on the performance for the rider.

order to be performed in an arena in front of a judge. The judge is there to comment in a constructive and helpful manner and award marks for the horse between 0 and 10 for each movement. After the test is finished, the judge will consider and award a mark for the rider's performance and writes a brief report on how the horse might be improved. Finally, all the points are added up and turned into a percentage that will determine who has won the competition.

Competitions are held at all levels from the amateur up to Olympic standard. Most amateur riders compete at preliminary, novice and elementary levels. Each level

is designed to progress the horse from balancing during the most basic corners and turns (preliminary), to showing more responsiveness and lengthening of strides (novice), to showing much higher levels of collection, accuracy and activity (elementary).

> **HINT**
>
> Brushing or tendon boots may be worn during the warmup but are not permitted when riding the test.

DRESSAGE TESTS

Competing in a dressage competition is a challenging yet enjoyable experience, especially if you have put in plenty of time beforehand working on the movements of the test and you have a chance of being placed.

To give yourself the best chance of success, choose a test that is slightly below the standard you are riding at home as nerves on the day can often lower the standard of your riding. In addition, allow yourself plenty of time to warm the horse up beforehand—how much time will depend on your horse but make sure it is supple and obedient enough to enter the arena but still has adequate energy to perform the test.

Anxiety may play a large part the first time you compete, so it is good practice to enter for two tests. The first test will give you the opportunity to work through the excitement of the day; for the second test, you should be able to be more focused and make the most of the event. For your first few competitions or if your nerves are likely to get the better of you, it is useful to have a helper to stand at the edge of the arena during your test and call out the movements while you are riding.

Five minutes before your test, you will be called to the ringside, where you can watch the test of the rider preceding you. When they have completed their test and left the arena, walk and trot your horse positively around the outside of the arena and gather your thoughts and concentration until the judge rings the bell for you to start. First impressions are everything, so

Judges really enjoy watching a horse and rider perform a good test, so **show off your horse** to its best advantage.

While waiting for the judge to ring the bell, use the time to focus and concentrate on your riding.

enter positively, smile and remember to keep breathing steadily, as this will encourage you and your horse to relax.

The judge will be awarding points for a good rhythm and balanced paces from the horse, particularly around corners, a nice forward way of going, submission by the horse to your aids, and your position and the effective use of your aids. The test must be ridden accurately with transitions made exactly at the markers requested.

Riding a dressage test in front of judges can be a daunting experience, so it is useful to exercise some mental control and make the most of the occasion. There may be other competitors riding in arenas on either side of you but try to ignore these and imagine

that it is just you putting on a show for the judge. Ride as if you are really showing off and present the best possible picture of you both at your best.

Dressage tests are designed to encourage riders to progress and all the marks and comments written on your score sheet are there to improve your riding technique.

HINT

Dressage is about your horse and you—so you need to look good, too.

153

CROSS-COUNTRY SCHOOLING

A prerequisite for cross-country schooling is the rider's ability to competently ride a galloping horse and be capable of jumping fences at speed. The aim of the cross-country event is to test the stamina, courage and ability of both you and your horse over a course that covers the open countryside, fields and woods. Obstacles are based on what might be found naturally when out riding in open territory, such as ditches, stone walls, fallen logs and water combinations. The important difference between show-jumping and cross-country fences is that cross-country fences are solid and will not

fall down if struck by the horse. With this in mind, you should tackle the fences boldly, transferring as much of that enthusiasm to the horse as possible so that it clears each obstacle with confidence while looking forward to the next.

The competition
In a competition environment, you must complete the course, which could be between 1 and 5 miles (1.5–8 km) long, within a given time limit. You will earn penalties if you ride the course too fast or too slow. Horses thoroughly enjoy riding across country in this manner but they must not be encouraged to gallop into fences. The real aim is to

Cross-country tests the stamina, courage and ability of both horse and rider.

Pay close attention to the layout of fences.

establish a strong rhythm for the duration of the course and yet have the ability to speed up or slow down according to the terrain.

Creating the right canter

To achieve the right canter, both you and your horse must trust each other and be extremely fit and strong. You must have plenty of core body strength, including well-muscled legs, in order to sit up and balance on your horse's back in jumping position for much of the ride. Cantering in the usual manner of sitting on the saddle would eventually tire the horse and possibly bruise its back.

Building confidence

Confidence should be built by tackling familiar obstacles, such as low walls, hedges and shallow water combinations, before jumping a combination of two, three or

more fences together to create that rhythm. Eventually you will have the confidence to jump quite a number of fences at once and to take them at a greater speed.

Walk the course

On the competition day, plan for enough time to walk the whole course before you ride. Pay close attention to the layout of each fence, especially where there are combinations. As well as memorizing the whole course, this will allow you to make quick decisions in the approach to fences to ensure you both clear them safely.

HINT

Pace is vital, switching from canter to gallop to jump, while keeping aware of the horse's energy and the clock.

LE TREC AND ENDURANCE

Inspections are undertaken during endurance rides to ensure that the horse is capable of completing the course.

Le Trec

Thirty years ago, France had a highly successful equestrian tourist business. Officials decided to adopt a more professional approach toward training and rating the many guides who worked within the industry. A system was designed to test the horse and rider on the broad range of activities they would encounter during an average trail ride—the result of which was Le Trec.

It soon became a very popular competition, with riders ranging from young children to adults. The concept has now gone worldwide and is an exciting new type of competition for North American riders.

Le Trec is made up of three phases:

- Phase one is to prove that the horse and rider can follow a predesignated route from reading a map and that they are capable of riding out all day over varied terrain.
- Phase two is to negotiate natural obstacles on the ride, such as riding under low branches, jumping natural obstacles and crossing over water, and to be able to dismount and leave the horse to stand alone for a period of time.
- Phase three concentrates on the welfare of the horse, making sure that the rider keeps the horse's best interests in mind throughout the ride and maintains respect for the countryside.

There are checkpoints at intervals during the ride where the progress of horse and rider are monitored carefully. Points are deducted or awarded for success in each phase and the winner is the horse and rider with the maximum number of points at the end of the day.

The overall aim of Le Trec is to enjoy riding horses in the open countryside. It is a real social sport as the horse and rider need a backup team to meet them at intervals during the day, which makes Le Trec an ideal sport for the whole family.

Endurance

Endurance riding is a much more intense sport than Le Trec and is not for the faint-hearted. Before the invention of modern-day transport, endurance or long-distance riding was done out of necessity rather than for fun. It may therefore seem ironic that, in the early 21st century, endurance riding has become the fastest-growing equestrian sport in the world.

Small rides begin at about 15 miles (25 km) and increase up to the ultimate distance of 100 miles (160 km) in a day—so the endurance provides something for everyone, whatever their aspirations. Similar to Le Trec, it is a very social sport with backup teams needed throughout the distance to provide food and water for both horse and rider.

Tactics on the longer rides are important as difficult terrain will lead to slower going at times, so riders need to concentrate on making up time in other ways. Much focus is given to training and keeping the horse in the best possible condition, so it is normal for horse and rider to develop a very strong bond with each other. Welfare is very important with all horses being fully vetted before, during and after the race to ensure that they are capable of the distance. Despite all its demands, endurance riding is renowned for being very friendly, as riders are competing against their own personal-best times rather than each other.

Le Trec tests the ability of horse and rider to negotiate various obstacles encountered on a ride.

The light build, stamina and balanced conformation of the Arab makes it an ideal horse for endurance riding.

RACING

Horse racing is often known as the "Sport of Kings" and has been practiced for centuries, with its roots dating back as far as Roman times. Popular the world over, it is keenly associated with gambling and, as a result, is very closely monitored by governing bodies. The type of racing varies according to the country it is based in—for example, in the United States quarter horse racing is extremely popular, while Great Britain is best known for hurdling and as the world center of thoroughbred racing. Flat racing (i.e., without jumps) is very popular in Australia, Hong Kong and the Middle East.

Horses are raced on tracks of either grass, which varies in its consistency according to the time of year and weather conditions, or a synthetic surface that remains the same

Racing is popular throughout the world— wherever people want to bet.

texture all year round. Distance is measured in furlongs, which equates to just over 200 yards, so a 5-furlong race would be almost 1 mile (1.6 km).

Hunt racing, or steeplechasing, is popular in many parts of the world and takes place over hurdles that are ridden at a gallop. Jockeys are often thrown—as much as one fall for every three races—but because of the speed that the horses are traveling, jockeys are usually thrown clear and will roll into a tight ball to protect themselves.

In racing, the horses' training and performance is everything. They must also be purebred, so much is made of their bloodlines and breeding, and a tremendous amount of thought goes into matching the right sire and dam when breeding foals.

DRIVING AND TROTTING

Negotiating obstacles in the marathon section demands skill and judgment from the driver.

Carriage driving

Carriage driving or combined driving, is a unique sport in that a 14-year-old girl can compete legitimately against a 70-year-old man. Both male and female competitors are welcome and, likewise, ponies and horses, although additional time assistance is given to very small ponies.

From one to eight horses are used at a time to pull the carriages. The driver is known as the "whip" and sits at the front of the carriage controlling the horses by using their voice and the reins and with light use of a driving whip. They are assisted by a groom or navigator who sits directly behind the driver and helps to balance the carriage by shifting their weight to the left and right as necessary.

Modeled on the traditional ridden three-day event, carriage driving consists of three stages over three days. Day one is the presentation and dressage phase where the vehicle, harness, driver and groom are judged on turn-out. The dressage test is similar to a ridden test and is designed to demonstrate control and obedience.

Day two is the marathon of approximately 6 miles (10 km) and consists of five timed sections. In the final section of the marathon, each obstacle on the course is negotiated at speed and demands enormous amounts of judgment and skill from the driver, making it a really thrilling spectator sport.

Day three is the cone-driving phase where the driver steers the horses at high speed through cones with a ball placed on top of each. Usually there are only inches to spare on either side of the carriage and, if a ball is displaced, penalties are incurred. This final stage requires total concentration and is the carriage driving equivalent to show-jumping.

Trotting

Trotting or harness racing is a century-old tradition and is as exhilarating as it is controversial. The horses are known as trotters if they move in the conventional diagonal trotting gait, or pacers if they trot with a lateral gait—moving both legs on each side at the same time. The driver balances astride a small lightweight carriage known as a "sulky" and uses his or her legs on each shaft to maintain an equilibrium.

A good trotter can cover 1 mile (1.6 km) in less than two minutes, which is a remarkable speed and equates almost to the pace of a galloping horse.

Similarly to jockeys, the drivers wear race colors to distinguish themselves and carry a long whip to encourage the horse forward. Because horses go faster on hard, flat surfaces than on grass, they are often illegally raced on roads in some parts of the world, which is considered dangerous for the horses as well as other road-users and also attracts unregulated betting. In other parts of the world, such as the United States and Canada, trotting or harness racing is well regulated, with competitions taking place on dirt tracks and officially monitored by governing bodies.

HACKING AND TRAIL RIDING

Hacking together with other horse-owners is a sociable way of exploring the countryside.

Hacking

Riding through the countryside at complete leisure is one of the most enjoyable equestrian activities and is done by a vast majority of riders. Both horse and rider can be relaxed with no pressure on them to accomplish a task or ride at any particular speed.

The ideal horse for hacking is calm, safe in traffic, responsive to the rider's commands but not overly so, and able to move easily over varying terrain. A further bonus is a long, effortless stride that makes for a more comfortable experience for the rider. A horse needs to be reasonably versatile for hacking in order to cope with the variety of challenges he might be faced with, for example, meeting heavy traffic during one part of the ride and then encountering farm animals or small obstacles at another part.

Riders can hack alone or with other horse-owners. This makes it more of a social experience, and is a great way of exploring the local countryside. Horse and rider normally start from their stables and ride through the surrounding area for as long as they wish. If a hacking route involves road work and there is the possibility of meeting a lot of traffic, it is advisable for the rider to wear high-visibility or reflective clothing to alert other road users of their presence in plenty of time so they can slow down and give the horse adequate space when passing.

Trail riding

Trail riding is a step up from hacking where the horses are ridden for up to 15 miles (25 km) a day following a predetermined route. Normally these are organized by a vacation company or riding stables, but trail riding can be done either alone, using maps, or with a specially hired guide to show the way. The routes are usually planned across country with little or no road work and you can expect to see some stunning scenery and plenty of wildlife along the way. Some riders will take their own horse on a trail ride in order to enjoy the experience together, but many people will ride a horse provided by the ranch and receive the necessary training before going out on the trail.

Some trail ride packages last for several days, so accommodation is included in the price— dinner and bed and breakfast are provided for the rider and either a stable or suitable field located nearby for the horse. On a properly organized trail ride, the luggage will be moved forward in advance and a packed lunch provided every day.

Longer and more advanced trail rides are not for novices, as at times the terrain may be challenging, and riders may need to dismount to tackle steeper pathways safely. But the rewards of riding your horse through unspoilt countryside, often in complete isolation, make it a rewarding experience.

When trail riding in the wilderness it is important to have a map or guide.

HOLIDAYS ON HORSEBACK

Your horse will be used to the region and familiar with the type of terrain.

A riding holiday is exactly as it sounds—a holiday dedicated to riding and being around horses. There is no better way to explore different environments than from the back of a horse, particularly as they are able to carry riders for miles along remote stretches to areas that are normally inaccessible by car. Riding holidays are available to suit every type of rider, from experienced jockeys who are able to cover long distances at speed to absolute beginners who would prefer simply to walk quietly for the whole ride.

Clothing for a riding holiday will be the same jodhpurs and riding boots that you wear at home, and although not all countries stipulate the use of hard hats, it is always good practice to take your own with you and wear it while mounted. At nighttime, you will either camp out like the locals would have done years ago, or stay at a properly equipped guest house to which your luggage will already have been forwarded. Rides can last from a couple of hours up to a full day, depending on what you have asked for, so expect to feel sore at first if you are not used to being in the saddle for such long periods. As a compensation, exploring new rides and getting to know new areas, or even other countries, like this is pure escapism and many find the fresh air and increase in their personal fitness invigorating.

Wherever you decide to go on your riding holiday, you will be in good hands because business owners take enormous pride in their knowledge of the landscape and the professionalism of their guides. The horses supplied will be native to their regions and familiar with whatever type of terrain is offered. They will also be used to carrying different riders, and it is not uncommon to form a strong bond with your allocated mount. All the horses are specially selected for their personality and endurance and at all times their welfare will be a priority. In Iceland, for example, at least double the quantity of horses needed are always taken on the ride to allow them sufficient rest from having a rider on their back. During their rest times they are unsaddled and follow the rest of the ride quite happily, making an enjoyable and unique experience for all who are taking part.

A riding holiday is a fantastic opportunity to ride in a different environment from the roads and tracks you are familiar with at home—for example, riding through the American Rockies where you could take part in a real cattle drive and watch the sun rise over a mountain range, or being able to gallop along a deserted sandy beach in France. A holiday on horseback can be a once-in-a-lifetime experience and a great chance to meet new, like-minded friends.

Riding holidays can offer a very different experience from your usual riding at home.

HORSE TRANSPORT

A horse correctly attired for traveling and ready to load.

When traveling with horses it is important to bear in mind how alien the concept is to them. They are transported among noisy traffic, enclosed on all sides, and almost totally restricted in movement with no idea of where they are going or how long it will take to get there. It is no surprise that some horses are reluctant to load into trailers and horseboxes or that some can travel very badly once they are on board.

Before loading, horses must be properly prepared for the journey with correctly fitted traveling boots, which are padded and cover well up the length of the leg, a tail bandage to protect the top of the tail from rubbing, a head collar, and lead rope. In addition to this,

during colder weather horses will often wear travel rugs that regulate their temperature while wicking away any sweat or moisture from the body.

There are two ways to transport horses: a specially designed horse trailer towed behind a normal family car or a horsebox.

Trailers

Trailers can carry up to two large horses facing forward and traveling side by side. They are loaded via a ramp at the rear of the trailer that is then raised and secured to form the back wall. For safety, a solid partition down the center separates both animals, with padded bars secured at chest height preventing them from moving forward or turning around. The floor is normally covered with non-slip rubber matting and ensures that the horses have plenty of grip during the journey. It is common practice to tie a haynet inside at the front of the trailer to keep the horses occupied during long distances. When towing a trailer, the driver must take extra care when turning corners and allow plenty of time to slow down at intersections. Providing the driver is smooth and steady, there is no reason for a horse to be unsettled during the experience, although the movements required by the horse to remain balanced and upright can be quite tiring and it may well need rest on arrival at the destination.

Horseboxes

A horsebox is much larger than a trailer and specially adapted to carry horses. Smaller horseboxes up to 7.5 tons can carry up to three horses or four ponies; larger horseboxes over 7.5 tons can carry up to eight horses. Again, horses are loaded into the rear of the horsebox but once on board are turned sideways and secured with a sturdy partition on either side. Some horses prefer travel in a horsebox, possibly because they feel more secure inside the larger environment. Competition horses and racehorses travel all

over the world in this manner, with modern versions becoming increasingly luxurious. Some specialized horseboxes also contain full living accommodation for the rider, including a small kitchen, and in some cases, a shower and toilet.

When loaded in a horsebox, horses stand sideways or on a slight diagonal with heads toward the rear.

A living area is really useful when staying away from home with your horse, such as for competitions or a weekend at the beach.

HOW THE HORSE EVOLVED

An Exmoor mare and foal. The breeding of horses today is, of course, heavily influenced by man.

For many years, the evolution of the horse was considered to have journeyed in a straight line with clear and simple moves from the earliest fossil horses to the modern-day *Equus*. However, further discoveries have shown that the evolution took place at different rates—some changes were very gradual, and others very dramatic.

Horse evolution was characterized by a reduction in the number of toes—from five per foot, to three per foot, to only one per foot. One of the first true horse species was the tiny *Hyracotherium*, which had four toes on each front foot and three toes on each hind foot. Over about five million years, these early equids evolved, with the fifth toe vanishing and new grinding teeth evolving. This was significant in that it signaled a transition to tougher plant material, allowing grazing of not just leafy plants but also tougher plants and grasses.

As the horse adapted to a drier, prairie environment, the second and fourth toes disappeared on all feet, and the horse became bigger. These side toes shrunk in and have vanished in the modern horse. All that remains are a set of small bones on either side of the cannon (the metacarpal and metatarsal bones, known informally as "splint bones," which are a frequent source of splints, a common injury in the modern horse).

The whole evolution is very detailed and is outside the span of this book but the main dates could be categorized as follows:

- The earliest *Equid* fossil dates to the Eocene period approximately 60 million years ago, when *Eohippus hyracotherium* inhabited the forest regions of North America.
- At the beginning of the late Eocene period, about 37 million years ago, there emerged three new types of horses: *Haplohippus*, *Mesohippus* and *Miohippus*.
- *Merychippus* emerged approximately 17 million years ago and would have been recognized as a horse as we know them today.
- *Equus* eventually evolved about four million years ago.

The horse became extinct in North America approximately 10 million years ago but continued to evolve in Europe and Asia. Four primitive breeds emerged about 6,000 years ago from which today's modern breeds developed:

- *The Asian wild horse* (also known as Przewalski's horse). Originally from the steppes of Asia, it was characterized by a heavy and long head with small eyes set high on the face, and was generally dun colored.
- *The tarpan.* Originally from eastern Europe, it was also dun colored and is credited with playing a large role in the development of the light horse of today.
- *The forest horse.* Originally from northern Europe, this horse was large-boned, heavy and slow-moving, and is believed to be an ancestor of the draft horse.
- *The tundra horse.* Originally from northeast Siberia.

From these four primitive breeds, four sub-species evolved by the time man began to domesticate the horse:
- *Pony Type 1.* Probably resembled the Exmoor pony and originated in northwest Europe.
- *Pony Type 2.* Thought to be similar to the Highland pony and originated in Eurasia.
- *Horse Type 3.* Its nearest modern-day equivalent is the Akhal-Teke and it originated in Central Asia.
- *Horse Type 4.* Probably resembled the Caspian and originated in west Asia.

Pony Type 2 is thought to have looked similar to this Highland pony.

Pony Type 1 probabaly resembled this Exmoor pony.

Horse Type 4 may have looked like this little Caspian pony.

The Akhal-Teke is thought to look like **Horse Type 3**.

> **HINT**
>
> Knowing about the history of the horse will increase your enjoyment of, and respect for, your animals.

HUMANS AND HORSES

Although logging has been carried out by steam and other more modern forms of transport, the **Shire horse** is still working in today's logging industries.

The horse has served humans for many years. Before the advent of motorized vehicles, horses were the main form of transport and also performed a variety of industrial tasks.

There are certain jobs that horses do very well, and no amount of technology appears able to supersede this. Mounted horses, for example, are used for effective crowd control by police forces in many countries. Cattle ranches still require riders on horseback to round up cattle that are scattered across remote, rugged terrain. In some countries, search and rescue organizations depend upon mounted teams to locate people, particularly hikers and hunters, who are lost in remote areas.

Some land management practices such as logging are handled more efficiently with horses. In areas such as nature reserves, they are used to avoid the disruption to delicate soil that would result from using vehicles. Forestry rangers may use horses for their patrols.

In many parts of the developing world, horses, donkeys and mules are widely used for transport and agriculture, especially for pulling plows or carts. Families often rely heavily on their animals to help them earn a living. In areas where roads are poor or nonexistent, fossil fuels are scarce, and the terrain rugged, riding horseback is still the most efficient way to get from place to place.

Heavy horses pulling the brewery drays (carts) were once a common sight in the city of London, England. These horses are still in evidence today at county shows, either performing carriage-driving demonstrations or showing the tradition of plowing.

Dating back to Roman times, horses were used as the main form of transport, carrying officers into battle ahead of the foot soldiers. During the First and Second World Wars, horses played a huge role, moving whole battalions many distances, displaying great courage and loyalty. They are still used today for many ceremonial duties and add to the pomp and ceremony of the occasion.

Mounted police working outside Buckingham Palace in London, England.

The Cadre Noir is an **equestrian display team** based in the city of Saumur in western France. The troop was founded in 1828 and gets its name from the black uniforms that are still used today.

171

HORSE BREEDS

Development of the horse

There are more than 150 different breeds and types of horses in the world, and their development has been greatly influenced by humans. Through domestication of the horse, humans introduced selective breeding and better-quality feeding. Both these practices resulted in increases in size and/or quality of the horse.

However, the biggest influence on the development of horse breeds was in response to the need of "form to function": that is, the need to acquire particular physical characteristics necessary to perform a certain type of work. Thus, light, refined horses such as the Arab developed in dry climates to be fast and have great endurance over long distances, while the heavy draft horse developed out of a need to pull plows. Ponies of all breeds developed out of a dual need to create mounts suitable for children as well as for work in small places such as mine shafts or in areas where there was insufficient forage to support larger draft animals.

The **Arab** is an example of a "hotblood" breed. This term refers to the horse's temperament. Hotblood breeds were developed for speed and endurance.

Breeding horses around the world

Some countries specialize in breeding horses suitable for particular activities. For example, the United States, Australia and regions of South America are known for breeding horses particularly suitable for working cattle and other livestock.

Germany produces Holsteiner and other "warmblood" breeds that are used particularly for dressage and show jumping. Ireland has always been well recognized for producing hunters and show-jumpers. Spain and Portugal are known for the Iberian horse, the Andalusian and Lusitano, used in dressage. Austria is known worldwide for its Lipizzaner horses, used for dressage and high-school work in the famous Spanish Riding School in Vienna. In Great Britain, there is an array of heavy draft horses and several breeds of hardy ponies, including the Dartmoor, New Forest and Welsh pony.

Both the United States and Great Britain are noted for breeding the thoroughbred for racing. Great Britain is well known for its heavy horse breed, the Shire. The United States also produces the Morgan and Quarter horse breeds, which are used extensively in Western riding pleasure classes.

The Shire is one of the "coldblood" breeds developed for heavy draft work.

The Hanoverian "warmblood" developed from crossing the hotblood and draft breeds to produce a versatile riding horse suitable for competitions.

BREEDS A–Z

BREEDS FROM EUROPE AND ASIA

Andalusian
Height: 15.1hh to 17hh.
Color: Usually gray (80 percent) but also black, bay, chestnut, roan coat with bay, palomino and buckskin.
Conformation: Handsome head; long, thick but elegant neck; short, strong body; rounded, strong hindquarters; medium-length, clean and strong limbs; long and luxuriant mane and tail.
Uses: High-school riding, dressage, parades.
Origin: Spain.

Arabian
Height: 14.1hh to 15hh.
Color: Mainly chestnut, bay and gray.
Conformation: A small head with a "dished" face; crested neck; long, sloping shoulder and short back; deep girth; strong hindquarters; the tail carried high and arched; hard, clean leg and short cannon bone.
Uses: General riding, showing, racing endurance.
Origin: Desert lands of Asia.

Caspian
Height: 10hh to 12hh.
Color: Traditionally bay, brown, chestnut, gray.
Conformation: Arabian-type head; long neck and shoulder; narrow body with short back; high-set tail; fine legs.
Uses: Primarily riding and driving.
Origin: The Middle East.

Connemara
Height: 13hh to 14hh.
Color: Predominantly gray but they can be black, brown or bay.
Conformation: An intelligent, well-carried head; medium-length neck on sloping shoulders; deep, compact body with strong, sloping hindquarters; short legs with good bone.
Uses: Riding—makes a good child's pony and is used for competition work.
Origin: Ireland.

The typically gray **Andalusian**.

Young **Icelandic** horses playing.

Dutch Warmblood
Height: 16hh to 17hh.
Color: Usually chestnut, bay, black or gray.
Conformation: Well-shaped head, usually with a straight profile; arched neck into sloping shoulders with pronounced withers; strong, straight and fairly long back, with short, broad and flat croup; powerful and muscular hindquarter with high-set tail; good, sound legs with good bone.
Uses: All-round competition horse.
Origin: The Netherlands.

Friesan
Height: Approximately 15hh.
Color: Always black.
Conformation: A fine, long head; crested neck; strong, compact body; rounded hindquarters; short legs with good bone and feathering; very full mane and tail.
Uses: Carriage horse and some draft work.
Origin: The Netherlands.

Haflinger
Height: 14hh.
Color: Chestnut or palomino with flaxen mane or tail.
Conformation: Intelligent head; strong, deep body with long back and muscular loins; powerful hindquarters; short legs with considerable bone.
Uses: An all-round riding and driving pony.
Origin: Austria.

Icelandic
Height: 12.3hh to 13.2hh.
Color: Any.
Conformation: Plain, heavy head; short neck; deep, compact body with short back; strong, muscular hindquarters; short legs.
Uses: Riding, pack and some draft work.
Origin: Iceland.

Lipizzaners from Austria in a military show.

Irish Draft
Height: 15.2hh to 17hh.
Color: Bay, brown, chestnut, gray.
Conformation: Intelligent head; thick neck; strong, deep body; powerful hindquarters; strong legs with good bone and little or no feather.
Uses: Hunter and some farm work. When crossed with the thoroughbred, produces good competition and riding horses.
Origin: Ireland.

Lipizzaner
Height: 15hh to 16hh.
Color: Born dark, but turning white or gray between 6 to 10 years. Occasionally bay.
Conformation: Small head; well-crested neck; longish body with good rib cage; strong hindquarters; legs have good bone.
Uses: Dressage, driving, some light farm work.
Origin: Austria, descended from Spanish horses.

Oldenburg
Height: 16.2hh and 17.2hh.
Color: Predominantly black, brown and bay.
Conformation: Plain head; long, strong neck; deep, powerful body; strong hindquarters; legs have plenty of bone.
Uses: Dressage and driving.
Origin: Germany.

Percheron
Height: 16hh and 17.2hh.
Color: Gray or black.
Conformation: Head wide across forehead; broad, deep chest; sloping shoulders; short, straight back; great depth in girth; long, wide hindquarters; short legs with flat, heavy bone.
Uses: Coach horse, riding, farming, warhorse.
Origin: La Perche in Normandy, France.

Selle Français
Height: About 16hh.
Color: Any, but predominantly chestnut.
Conformation: Refined head; long neck; deep chest; strong body with well-sprung ribs; powerful hindquarters; good legs.
Uses: A good competition horse, particularly for show-jumping, eventing and general riding.
Origin: France.

Trakhener
Height: 16hh to 16.2hh.
Color: Any solid color, usually dark.
Conformation: An attractive head; long neck and prominent withers; strong, medium body; well-rounded hindquarters; hard legs with good feet.
Uses: Good action, conformation and a spirited temperament combine to make Trakheners excellent competition and general riding horses.
Origin: Germany.

The German Trakhener

The Selle Français, a great competition horse.

BREEDS FROM THE AMERICAS

Appaloosa

Height: 14.2hh to 16hh.

Color: There are six main Appaloosa patterns (no two horses are alike) and several pattern variations. Roan is the most common base color. Any color is accepted if the pattern conforms to one of six categories:

- Leopard—all-over white background, dark spots.
- Snowflake—all-over dark background, white spots.
- Spotted blanket—mainly dark body, dark spots on white back and/or hindquarters.
- White blanket—mainly light body, dark back and/or hindquarters.
- Marble—dark coat at birth, fades to almost white as horse grows older, except for a few darker markings on legs and face.
- Frosted tip—dark background, light-colored or white spots on loins/hips.

Conformation: A compact type with well-shaped neck; short back and powerful quarters; strong limbs; good, hard feet.

Uses: Pleasure, Western, show, halter, youth, cow pony classes.

Origin: United States.

Criollo

Height: 14hh to 15hh.

Color: Mainly dun with dark points and dorsal strip; sometimes roan, chestnut or bay.

Conformation: A short, broad head; muscular neck; strong shoulders and broad chest; deep body; fine strong legs with small feet.

Uses: Ranch work; when crossed with the thoroughbred, make good polo ponies.

Origin: Argentina.

Falabella

Height: under 7hh high, averaging 30 to 32.5 in (75–80 cm) at the withers, but some can be as small as 23 in (58 cm).

Color: Most.

Conformation: Proportioned like a miniature horse; fine bones and small feet. While the Falabella is very small, it is not a pony but a miniature horse because its conformation is similar to that of a horse.

Uses: Pets and in harness.

Origin: Argentina.

BREEDS A–Z

Morgan
Height: 14.1hh to 15.2hh.
Color: Bay, brown, black, chestnut. No white markings permitted above the knee or hock, except on the face.
Conformation: Small head with a slightly concave profile; slightly arched neck; compact, deep body; well-muscled hindquarters with high-set tail; straight, sound legs.
Uses: A versatile all-round riding and driving horse.
Origin: United States.

FACT

The English settlers in North America raced the quarter horse over stretches of about a quarter mile, hence the name.

Quarter horse
Height: 15hh to 16hh.
Color: Any solid color, but usually chestnut.
Conformation: Short head; long, flexible neck; compact body with deep girth and broad chest; well-muscled hindquarters; good legs.
Uses: Western, ranch work, endurance, racing, jumping, hunting, polo.
Origin: United States.

A beautifully proportioned **Quarter horse**.

The **Saddlebred** with unique conformation.

The saddlebred's classic trot.

Saddlebred

Height: 15hh to 16hh.
Color: Black, brown, bay, gray and chestnut.
Conformation: Well-shaped head; long, arched neck; short, strong back; well-muscled hindquarters with high-set tail; straight, strong legs.
Uses: Mainly under saddle or in harness in the show ring but some general riding.
Origin: United States.

> **FACT**
>
> The saddlebred can be three-gaited (walk, trot and canter) or five-gaited (also performing a four-beat, slow gait and the rack—a fast, flashy, four-beat gait).

BREEDS A-Z

BREEDS FROM GREAT BRITAIN
Cleveland Bay
Height: 16hh to 16.2hh.
Color: Bay with black points.
Conformation: Large head; long, lean neck; a long, deep, wide body; short, strong, clean legs.
Uses: Riding and driving; produces excellent hunters and competition horses when crossed with the thoroughbred.
Origin: Great Britain.

Dales
Height: 14hh to 14.2hh.
Color: Predominantly black, can be bay or brown and occasionally gray.
Conformation: A neat head on a strong neck; a powerful, compact body; thick mane and tail; short legs with feathering on the feet.
Uses: All-round riding and driving pony.
Origin: The eastern side of the Pennine Hills in Great Britain.

Dartmoor
Height: Not exceeding 12.2hh.
Color: Normally bay, brown or black.
Conformation: A small head with very small ears; a strong neck on shoulders set well back; strong hindquarters with a high-set, full tail; slim, hard legs.
Uses: Traditionally used as a child's pony.
Origin: Great Britain.

Fell pony
Height: 13hh to 14hh.
Color: Predominantly black, can be brown and bay and occasionally gray.
Conformation: An alert head on a strong neck; a short-coupled, deep body with strong hindquarters; good legs with plenty of bone; feathering on the feet; a thick mane and tail.
Uses: Primarily riding, driving, and trekking.
Origin: The western side of the Pennine Hills in Great Britain.

New Forest
Height: 13.2hh to 14.2hh.
Color: Any except skewbald and piebald.
Conformation: Well-set-on head; short neck; good shoulder; deep body; strong hindquarters; straight legs.
Uses: General riding.
Origin: Great Britain.

Shetland
Height: 7hh to 11hh.
Color: Black is the foundation color, but any except spotted.
Conformation: Small head; strong, deep body with short back and muscular loins; strong legs; profuse mane and tail.
Uses: As the smallest of the British native breeds, the Shetland is mainly

A **Shetland**, much loved by children.

A **New England Shire**, an intelligent and hard-working animal.

used as a child's pony but it is also a good driving pony.
Origin: Shetland Isles, Great Britain.

Shire
Height: 16.3hh to 18hh.
Color: Bay, brown or black; chestnut is rare.

Conformation: Intelligent head with wide muzzle and large nostrils; long, arched neck; short back with well-sprung ribs; muscular hindquarters; straight legs with great bone and feather.
Uses: Draft work and showing.
Origin: Great Britain.

Suffolk Punch
Height: 16hh to 16.3hh.
Color: Always chestnut.
Conformation: Large head; deep, tapering
neck; long, muscular shoulders; deep,
well-rounded body; strong quarters; short,
straight legs with plenty of bone and
no feathers.
Uses: Draft work and showing.
Origin: Suffolk, Great Britain.

Suffolk Punch: Some
are still working but
not commercially.

The **Thoroughbred**: The name says it all.

Thoroughbred
Height: 16hh to 16.2hh.
Color: Any solid color.
Conformation: Variable but refined head;
elegant, arched neck; back not too long with
deep, well-sprung ribs; muscular hindquarters
with well-set tail; clean, hard legs.
Uses: Racing, eventing, hunting, general
riding; crosses well with horses of substance
to produce quality hunters, hacks, polo ponies.
Origin: Great Britain.

> **FACT**
>
> The Thoroughbred developed in
> England in the 17th and 18th centuries.
> It descends from three Eastern sires: the
> Byerley Turk, the Darley Arabian and the
> Godolphin Barb.

Welsh

The Welsh pony and cob are divided into four sections: A, B, C and D.

Welsh Mountain Pony (Section A)
Height: Not exceeding 12hh.
Color: Any solid color.
Conformation: Small, clean-cut head; lengthy, well-carried neck; long, sloping shoulders; strong, muscular back with deep girth; lengthy, fine hindquarters; good, strong legs with some feather.
Uses: Excellent children's pony, good trot, goes well in harness.
Origin: Wales, Great Britain.

Welsh Pony (Section B)
Similar to the Welsh Mountain Pony but larger—not exceeding 13.2hh.

Welsh Pony—Cob Type (Section C)
Height: Not exceeding 13.2hh.
Color: Any solid color.
Conformation: Quality head, lengthy, well-carried neck; strong, well-laid-back shoulders; strong, deep muscular body; muscular hindquarters with high-set tail; short, powerful legs.
Uses: Farm work, general riding, driving, showing.

Welsh Cob (Section D)
A slightly larger version of the cob-type pony, with a height of 14hh to 15.1hh.

FACT

The Welsh Mountain Pony is thought to have evolved from the prehistoric Celtic pony, with the inhospitable hills of Wales influencing an extremely hardy animal. It is believed that these native ponies bred with Arabians brought to Britain during the Roman occupation.

Versatile and popular **Welsh ponies.**

GLOSSARY OF TERMS

A

action: The movement of the horse's legs.

aids: Signals or cues by which the rider communicates with the horse.

B

bascule: Term used to describe the arc a horse makes as it jumps.

bay: Coat color—deep reddish brown with black mane and tail.

bit: Mouthpiece made of metal, rubber or other synthetic material and held in place by the bridle, by which the rider conveys instructions to the horse.

breed: An equine group bred selectively for consistent characteristics over a long period of time.

bridle: Item of equipment worn on the horse's head, enabling the rider to communicate his or her wishes through use of the bit and the reins.

bridoon: Snaffle bit used in conjunction with a curb bit in a double bridle.

C

canter: Three-beat gait of the horse. Similar to the lope in Western riding.

cantle: back ridge of an English saddle.

cavesson: Simple noseband fitted to a bridle. Leather or nylon headgear, with attachments for side reins and lunge line, worn by the horse when being lunged.

cinch: Strap by which a Western saddle is secured to the horse. Called a girth in English riding.

conformation: The way in which a horse is put together and also the relationship of specific parts of the horse in regards to its proportions.

cow hocks: Hocks turned in like those of a cow.

curb bit: Bit fitted with cheeks and a curbchain that lies in the chin groove. Operates on the leverage principle acting on the lower jaw. In a double bridle, the curb bit is used in conjunction with a bridoon, or snaffle bit.

D

diagonals: At the trot, the horse's legs move in diagonal pairs, called diagonals. When on a circle, the rider rises as the outside foreleg moves forward.

double bridle: Traditional English bridle with two bits (snaffle and curb) giving the rider a greater degree of control than a single bit.

dropped or drop noseband: Noseband that buckles beneath the bit to prevent the horse from opening its mouth and ignoring the rider's rein aids.

E

eventing: Equestrian competition held over one or three days. Includes the disciplines of dressage, cross-country and show-jumping.

F

farrier: Skilled craftsperson who shoes horses.

feathers: Long hair on the lower legs and fetlocks. Abundant on heavy horse breeds.

fetlock: Lowest joint on the horse's leg.

flexion: When the horse yields the lower jaw to the bit, with the neck bent at the poll. Also describes the full bending of the hock joints.

forehand: The horse's head, neck, shoulder, withers and forelegs. Horses in lower levels of training, who have not yet learned to balance themselves in self-carriage and are heavy in the bridle, are said to be on the forehand.

forelock: The mane between the ears that hangs forward over the forehead.

frog: Triangular, rubber pad on the sole of the foot that acts as a shock absorber.

G

gait: The paces at which horses move, usually the walk, trot, canter and gallop.

gallop: Four-beat gait of the horse.

girth: (i) The circumference of the body measured from behind the withers around the barrel; (ii) means by which an English saddle is secured to the horse. Called a cinch in Western riding.

grackle noseband: Noseband with thin leather straps that cross over at the front and buckle both above and below the bit.

grooming kit: The various brushes, combs and other equipment used to clean the horse's coat, mane, tail and hooves.

H

half-halt: An exercise used to communicate to the horse that the rider is about to ask for some change of direction or gait, or other exercise or movement.

hand: Unit of measurement used to describe the height of a horse.

harness: The equipment of a horse that is driven, as opposed to ridden.

heavy horse: Any large draft horse, such as the Shire, Clydesdale, or Belgian Draft.

hindquarters: That part of the horse's body that extends from the rear of the flank back to the top of the tail and down to the top of the gaskin.

hock: Joint midway up the hind leg, responsible for providing most of the forward energy of the horse.

horn: (i) Hard, insensitive outer covering of the hoof; (ii) prominent pommel at the front of a Western saddle.

I

inside leg: The legs of horse and rider that are on the inside of any circle.

irons: The metal pieces attached to the saddle by means of leather straps in which the rider places their feet.

J

jog: Western riding term for trot.

GLOSSARY OF TERMS

L

laminitis: Condition, caused by systemic upset, in which the laminae inside the hoof become inflamed and painful to the horse.

lead: The horse's leading leg in canter.

leg up: Method of mounting in which an assistant stands behind the rider and supports the lower part of their left leg, giving a boost as necessary as the rider springs off the ground.

lope: Slow Western canter.

lunge: (i) The act of training a horse by working it in the various paces on a circle using a long lunge rein; (ii) riders may have lessons on the lunge as they learn the basics of position, without having to concern themselves with the control of the horse.

M

manege: An enclosure used for training and schooling horses. Also called a school.

martingale: Item of tack used to prevent the horse from raising its head above the level of the rider's hand and evading the rein aids.

mucking out: Daily stable chore that involves the removal of wet and soiled bedding and general tidying of the stable.

N

nearside: The left-hand side of the horse.

neck reining: The art of turning the horse by using the indirect, or opposite, rein against the neck.

O

offside: The right-hand side of the horse.

on the bit: When a horse carries its head in a near vertical position and calmly accepts the rider's contact on the reins.

P

pastern: The sloping bone in the lower leg that connects the hoof to the fetlock.

pelham: Curb bit with a single mouthpiece to which two reins may be attached.

poll: The highest point on the top of the horse's head.

pommel: The center front of an English saddle.

Q

quarters: The part of the horse's body from the rear of the flank to the top of the tail down to the top of the gaskin. Also called the hindquarters.

quidding: A horse that drops partially chewed food from its mouth, usually because of age or dental problems.

R

reining: Type of Western riding in which advanced movements such as spins and slides are executed in various patterns.

rising trot: The action of the rider rising from the saddle in rhythm with the horse's trot.

S

school: Enclosed, marked-out area used for the training and exercise of the horse. Also called a manege.

serpentine: School movement in which the horse, at any pace, moves down the school in a series of equal-sized loops.

side reins: Reins used in training to help position the horse's head. They attach at one end to the bit, and to the girth or training surcingle at the other end.

snaffle (bit): Design of bit that acts on the corners or bars of the horse's mouth. May be jointed or straight, but does not have shanks and only uses one rein.

sound: Free from lameness or injury.

surcingle: Webbing strap that passes around the horse's barrel. Can be used to attach side reins to when lunging young horses.

T

tack: The equipment of a riding horse—saddle, bridle and so on.

transition: The act of changing from one pace to another.

trot: Moderate-speed gait in which the horse moves from one diagonal pair of legs to the other, with a period of suspension in between.

U

unsoundness: Term used to describe any condition or conformation fault that limits the horse's ability to perform its job.

W

withers: Point at the bottom of the horse's neck from which the horse's height is measured.

INDEX

INDEX/ACKNOWLEDGEMENTS

The Author and Publishers are grateful to the following for their help in producing this book: All the staff at Flawborough Equine, Mickey Gavin, Catherine Arden, Patrick Stubbs, Carrie Adams, Janice; the Keeble Cottage Equestrian Centre team of Claire Catley, Nicky Somers, Roberta Cornish and Emma Clark. Special thanks also go Janice Baiton.

The photographs are: ©Bob Langrish Photography, www. boblangrish.com: Title page; p.6; p.12 both; p.13 both; p.16; p.17 t; p.31 spurs; p.40; p.60; p.62; p.63; p.71; p.72; p.74; p.75; p.81 t; p.82; p.83 b; p.85 b; p.91; p.92; p.93 t; p.98; p.99; p.101; p.102 both; p.104; p.105 t, br, and inset; p.106; p.107 t; p.108; p.109; p.111 tr; p.116; p.117 both; p.118; p.121; p.122; p.123; p.135; p.136; p.137; p.138; p.139; p.140; p.141 both; p.142; p.143 t; p.145 all; p.146; p.147 both; p.148 both; p.149; p.150; p.151; p.152; p.153; p.154; p.156; p.157 both; p.158/159; p.160; p.161; p.163; p.164; p.165; p.168; p.169 all; p.170; p.171 both; p.172; p.173 both; p.174; p.175; p.176 both; p.177; p.178; p.179 both; p.180; p.181; p.182 both; p.183; p.185; back cover. ©Corbis: p.125. ©Daniel Berehulak/Reportage/Getty Images: p.97 b. ©Z.

Molesworth: p.134. © Natural Expressions Photography, www. naturalexpressions.co.uk: Front cover; Imprint page; Contents page; p.7; p.8; p.9; p.10; p.11; p.14; p.15 both; p.17 b; p.18 both; p.19 t; p.20; p.21 both; p.22; p.23; p.24 all; p.25 all; p.26; p.27 all; p.28; p.29 all; p.30 all; p.31 martingales; p.32 both; p.33 all; p.34 all; p.35 all; p.36; p.37 both; p.38 both; p.39 both; p.41; p.42; p.43 all; p.44; p.45; p.46; p.48 both; p.49 all; p.50 all; p.51 both; p.52; p.53 all; p.54; p.55 all; p.56 all; p.57 all; p.58 both; p.59 both; p.64; p.65; p.66; p.67; p.68; p.69 both; p.70 both; p.73; p.76; p.77 all; p.78; p.79; p.80; p.81 b; p.83 t; p.84; p.85 t; p.90 both; p.93 b; p.94; p.95 all; p.96; p.97 br; p.103; p.105 bl; p.110 both; p.111 bl; p.112 ; p.113 both; p.114; p.115 both; p.119 both; p.120; p.124; p126; p.127 all; p.128 both; p.129; p.130; p.131 both; p133 both; p.143 b l and r; p.144 all; p.154; p.162; p.166; p.167 both; Glossary all.

Illustrations are by Tony Wilkins

Editorial, layout and production by Hart McLeod limited, Cambridge.